MAXIMIZE YOUR BRAINPOWER

Titles in *The IQ Workout Series*

Psychometric Testing: 1000 ways to assess your personality, creativity, intelligence and lateral thinking 0-471-52376-3

Increase Your Brainpower: Improve your creativity, memory, mental agility and intelligence 0-471-53123-5

IQ Testing: 400 ways to evaluate your brainpower
0-471-53145-6

More IQ Testing: 400 new ways to release your IQ potential
0-470-84717-4

The IQ Workout Series

MAXIMIZE YOUR BRAINPOWER

1000 new ways to boost your mental fitness

Philip Carter and Ken Russell

JOHN WILEY & SONS, LTD

Published in 2002 by John Wiley & Sons Ltd,
Baffins Lane, Chichester,
West Sussex PO19 1UD, England

National   01243 779777
International   (+44) 1243 779777
e-mail (for orders and customer service enquiries):
cs-books@wiley.co.uk
Visit our Home Page on http://www.wiley.co.uk
or http://www.wiley.com

Reprinted March 2003

Other Wiley Editorial Offices

John Wiley & Sons, Inc., 605 Third Avenue,
New York, NY 10158-0012, USA

WILEY-VCH Verlag GmbH, Pappelallee 3,
D-69469 Weinheim, Germany

John Wiley & Sons Australia Ltd, 33 Park Road, Milton,
Queensland 4064, Australia

John Wiley & Sons (Asia) Pte Ltd, 2 Clementi Loop #02-01,
Jin Xing Distripark, Singapore 129809

John Wiley & Sons (Canada) Ltd, 22 Worcester Road,
Rexdale, Ontario M9W 1L1, Canada

British Library Cataloguing in Publication Data

A catalogue record for this book is available from the British Library

ISBN 0-470-84716-6

Typeset in 11/14 pt Garamond Book by Dorwyn Ltd, Rowlands Castle, Hants.
Printed and bound in Great Britain by Biddles Ltd, Guildford and King's Lynn.

This book is printed on acid-free paper responsibly manufactured from sustainable forestry, in which at least two trees are planted for each one used for paper production.

Contents

Introduction

There is no man living who isn't capable of doing more
than he thinks he can do.

Henry Ford

Every production of genius must be the production of
enthusiasm.

Benjamin Disraeli

Despite the enormous capacity of the human brain, we only
use on average 2% of our potential brainpower. This is the
amount of information available to us consciously, and the
rest is locked within our subconscious mind. There
is, therefore, the potential for each of us to expand our
brainpower considerably.

This book sets out to show that by regular practice on
different types of tests and puzzles each one of us has the
capacity to maximize our brainpower and strengthen our
performance at different types of brain activity. Just as
gymnasts are able to improve their performance, and increase
their chances of success, at whatever level they are competing,
by means of punishing training schedules and refinement of
technique, in the same way this book provides the reader with
a series of mental workouts covering areas of creative thinking,
problem solving, memory, logical thought and mental agility.

Most of us take our brain for granted, believing there is little
we can do to improve the brain we have been born with. Also,

because we know so little about the human brain, there is the fear factor – the fear of the unknown that we do not even like to think about, let alone talk about – however, the brain is the most vital organ in the human body and our most valuable asset. It gives rise to our perceptions and memory, and it shapes our speech, skills, thoughts and feelings, yet it is perhaps the part of our body which we tend to neglect the most.

In the past few decades we have become much more aware of the importance of the human brain, its functioning and its relationship to our body, in fact, we have learned more about the brain in the past decade or so than in all of the previous centuries.

We are now becoming more aware than ever that we all have the capacity to put our brain to even more use by exploring new avenues, experiences and learning adventures. It is our hope that this book, a follow-up to our earlier volume, *Increase Your Brainpower*, will go some way to boosting the brain potential, increasing the confidence and unleashing much untapped creativity of many of our readers.

About the brain

Study of other animals suggests a relationship exists between brain size and intelligence levels. The dolphin, for example, has an unusually large brain and is considered one of our planet's most highly intelligent creatures. Human brain size levelled off about 100,000 years ago. Unlike animals, there is no relationship between brain size and intelligence level in humans. When it comes to human brain size, therefore, bigger is not necessarily better. In fact, scientists believe bigger could be worse, because increased size may impede rapid communication between nerve cells within the brain.

In vertebrates the brain is the portion of the central nervous system within the skull. Often referred to as *grey matter* it is, in humans, a mass of pink-grey tissue and weighs approximately 1.3 kg (3 lb).

The brain is the control centre for virtually every vital activity necessary for survival including movement, sleep, hunger and thirst. In addition, all human emotions including love, hate, anger, elation and sadness are controlled by the brain. It also receives and processes signals that are sent to it from other parts of the body and from sources external to the body.

The brain comprises three distinct but connected parts: the cerebrum, the cerebellum and the brain stem. The largest part of the brain is the cerebrum which makes up approximately 85% of the brain's weight. It has a large surface area called the cortex and is divided by a fissure into identical right and left hemispheres. The cerebrum is responsible for many vital functions including speech, smell, hearing, behaviour, vision and memory.

The cerebellum lies at the back part of the cranium and is composed of two hemispheres connected by white fibres called the vermis. The cerebellum is essential to the control of movement and acts as a reflex centre for co-ordination and maintenance of equilibrium.

The brain stem is made up of all the structures lying between the cerebrum and the spinal cord and is divided into several components which regulate, or are involved in, many vital activities necessary for survival. These include, for example, eating, drinking, temperature regulation, sleep, emotional behaviour, sexual activity and cardiac and respiratory functions.

Oxygen and glucose are supplied to the brain by two sets of cranial arteries known as the vascular system. Of all the blood pumped by the heart, 25% is circulated within the brain tissue by a large network of cerebral and cerebellar arteries.

Communication in the brain takes the form of electrical impulses which run along pathways connecting the various sectors. These connections are formed by a group of dendroids which are threadlike extensions that grow out of neurons, the specialized cells of the nervous system. As well as dendroids, neurons have extensions called axons. Dendrites bring information to the cell body and axons take information away from the cell body.

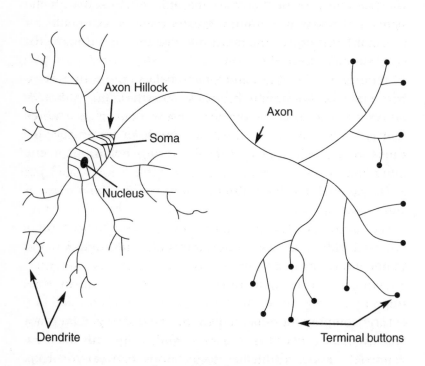

Composition of a neuron

Each neuron is a cell that uses biochemical reactions to receive, process and transmit information, or messages, through an electrochemical process.

The branches of a neuron's dendrite (the dendritic tree) are connected to a thousand neighbouring neurons. It is when one of these neurons fire that a positive or negative charge is received by one of the dendrites. The strengths of all the charges are added together and the aggregate input is then passed to the soma, the cell body. The primary function of the soma and its nucleus is not the processing of incoming and outgoing data but is to perform the continuous maintenance required to keep the neuron functional. It is the axon hillock which is the part of the soma that concerns itself with the signal. If the aggregate input is greater than the axon hillock's threshold, this causes the neuron to fire and an output signal is transmitted down the axon.

Neurons are the oldest and longest cells in the body and we have many of the same neurons for our whole life. Although other cells die and are replaced, many neurons are never replaced when they die, therefore, we have fewer neurons when we are old compared to when we are young. On the other hand data published in the late 1990s shows that in at least one area, the hippocampus, new neurons can grow in adult humans.

The more connections there are between the brain's hundred billion neurons, the more efficiently it will work. Connections form as a result of two elements: inherited growth patterns, and in response to external and internal stimuli.

Large amounts of brain activity, the kind that goes on in a healthy and active brain, can stimulate growth of new dendroids, fostering further connections between neurons and improving overall brain functioning.

In addition to 100 billion neurons, there are about 10 to 50 times that many glial cells in the brain, in fact, these small cells account for about half the brain's weight and are now sometimes referred to as the brain's housekeepers.

Traditionally, glia has been thought of as mere support for the brain's neural network, however, scientists are now discovering that glial cells may play a much greater role in the brain's communication than previously thought. Although glial cells do not carry nerve impulses, they do have many important functions without which neurons would not work properly. These include providing physical and nutritional support for neurons by cleaning up brain debris, transporting nutrients to neurons, holding neurons in place, digesting parts of dead neurons, providing insulation to neurons in the central nervous system and peripheral nervous system and providing physical support to neurons in the peripheral nervous system.

Although research into the importance of glial cells is still in its infancy, neurobiologists have demonstrated that, by themselves, pure populations of nerve cells and glia connect together poorly, however, the combination of the two cell types result in strong connections between nerve cells. In the brain such connections allow nerve cells to transmit messages about activities such as thought, memory and movement, however, the weakening of these connections could be responsible for memory loss, symptoms of strokes and Alzheimer's disease.

The human brain is an infinitely complex subject and these complexities are, and will continue to be, the subject of much debate. As technological methods become more advanced, and our knowledge of the functions of the brain increases, these issues will be increasingly revealed, as will treatments for abnormal diseases of the brain such as strokes, brain disorders, Parkinson's disease and cerebral palsy.

If you have any questions about the tests included in this, or any of the other books in the IQ Workout Series, please email us at: iqworkoutseries@wiley.co.uk.

1

Creativity

If we were to remove a brain from the skull we would see that it is made up of two almost identical hemispheres. These two hemispheres are connected by a bridge, or interface, of millions of nerve fibres called the corpus callosum which allows them to communicate with each other. Thus, the human brain consists of three main parts, the left hemisphere, the right hemisphere and the all-important interface between these two hemispheres.

In order to work to its full potential, each of these hemispheres must be capable of analysing its own input first, only exchanging information with the other half, by means of the interface, when a considerable amount of processing has taken place.

Because both hemispheres are capable of working independently, human beings are able to process two streams of information at once. The brain then compares and integrates the information to obtain a broader and more in-depth understanding of the concept under examination.

In the early 1960s the American psychologist Roger Sperry showed by a series of experiments, first using animals whose corpus callosum had been severed, and then on human patients whose corpus callosum had been severed in an attempt to cure epilepsy, that each of the two hemispheres has developed specialized functions and has its own private sensations, perceptions, ideas and thoughts, all separate from the opposite hemisphere. As their experiments continued, Sperry, who won the 1981 Nobel Prize for medicine for his work in this area, and his team were able to reveal much more about how the two hemispheres were specialized to perform different tasks.

For most people the left side of the brain is analytical and functions in a sequential and logical fashion and is the side which controls language, academic studies and rationality. On the other hand, the right side is *creative* and intuitive and leads, for example, to the birth of ideas for works of art and music.

This is where the interface between the two halves of the brain becomes so important. In order for the subconscious of the right-hand hemisphere to function, it needs the fuel, in other words data, which has been fed into, collated and processed by the left-hand hemisphere.

The real danger is the overburdening of the left-hand hemisphere with too much data, and too quickly, to the extent that the creative side of the brain is unable to function to its full potential. On the other hand, lack of data fed into the left-hand hemisphere could result in the creative side, or right-hand hemisphere, drying up. It is, therefore, desirable to strike the right balance between right and left hemispheres in order for the brain to work to its full potential. The term *creativity* refers to mental processes that lead to solutions, ideas, concepts, artistic expression, theories or products that are unique and novel. Because it is such a diverse subject in which there are so many different ways in which creativity manifests itself, and because in so many people it is to a great extent unexplored, creativity is very difficult, if not impossible, to measure.

The French mathematicians Poincaré and Hadamard defined the following four stages of creativity:

1 Preparation   – the attempt to solve a problem by normal means.

2 Incubation   – when you feel frustrated that the above methods have not worked and as a result you then move on to other things.

3 Illumination – the answer suddenly comes to you in a flash via your subconscious.

4 Verification – your reasoning powers take over as you analyse the answer which has come to you, and you assess its feasibility.

The right-hand hemisphere of the human brain, which controls the creative functions, is the side of the brain which is under-used by the majority of people. Because it is under-used, much creative talent in many people remains untapped throughout their life. Until we try, most of us never know what we can achieve, for example, one in three people in Britain have the desire to write a novel, yet only a very small percentage of these people progress any further than the initial stage of just thinking about it.

We all have a creative side to our brain, therefore we all have the potential to be creative. However, because of the pressures of modern living and the need for specialization, many of us never have the time or opportunity, or indeed are given the encouragement, to explore our latent talents, even though most of us have sufficient ammunition to realize this potential in the form of data which has been fed into, collated and processed by the brain over many years.

Writers, indeed all artists, must, therefore, use both halves of the brain. They must use the right side of the brain to create things, and the left side of the brain to organize things. The creative and intuitive right side is able to cope with complexity and this is where insights originate, whilst the left side controls language, academic studies and rational intellectual work. The problem is, especially as in so many people the left half of the brain is possessively dominant, getting these two halves of the brain to pass information back and forth and work together.

In order to perform any creative task it is necessary to encourage your right side to start its creative juices flowing, in other words, move your mental processes, albeit temporarily, from the dominant left side across to the creative right side. This may sound an easy enough task in theory, but not so easy to put into practice.

Like many other tasks, or pleasures, the majority of us never know what we can achieve until we try. Having then tried, we instinctively know whether we find it enjoyable or whether we have a talent or flair for it. Then, if these signs are positive, we persevere. By cultivating new leisure activities and pursuing new pastimes it is possible for each of us to exploit the potential and often vastly under-used parts of the human brain.

The following exercises, while different in themselves, are all designed with the object of improving or recognizing your own powers of mental productivity, generation of ideas and artistic skills.

Tests of creativity

Progressive matrices test (Answers, see pp. 167–8)

The ten questions here are designed to test and exercise your appreciation of pattern and design, your ability to think laterally and to explore with an open mind the various possibilities that might lead to a correct solution.

In tests of intelligence, a matrix is an array of squares in which one of the squares has been omitted, and where you must choose the correct missing square from a number of options. It is, therefore, necessary to study the matrix to decide what pattern is occurring, either by looking across each line and down each column, looking at the array as a whole or looking at the relationship between different squares within the array.

The test that follows consists of ten questions which gradually increase in difficulty as the test progresses, first starting with 2 × 2 arrays, then 3 × 3 arrays and finally 4 × 4 arrays. The tests call for a great deal of creative right-brain thinking and you must apply your mind to each set of diagrams in order to appreciate the patterns and sequences that are occurring.

You have 45 minutes in which to solve the ten questions.

1   (i)

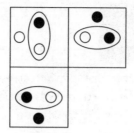

Which is the missing square?

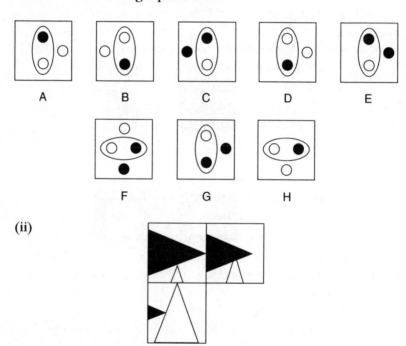

A   B   C   D   E

F   G   H

(ii)

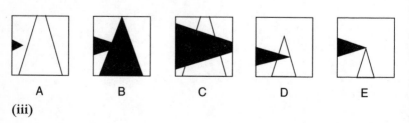

Which is the missing square?

A   B   C   D   E

(iii)

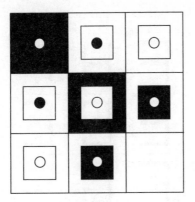

Which is the missing square?

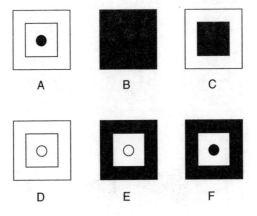

(iv)

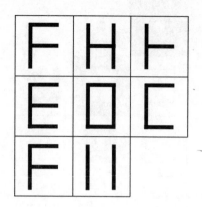

Which is the missing square?

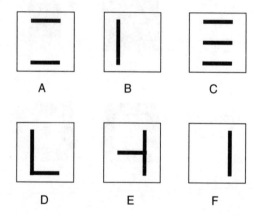

(v)

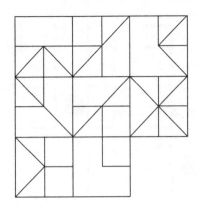

Which is the missing square?

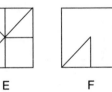

A   B   C

D   E   F

(vi)

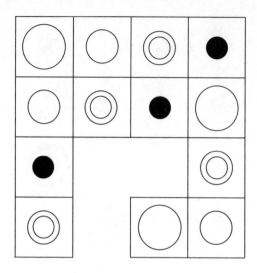

Which is the missing section?

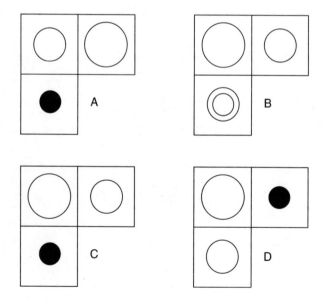

(vii)

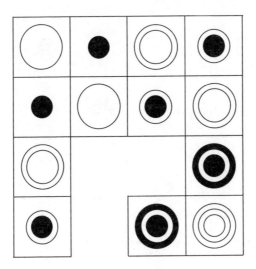

Which is the missing section?

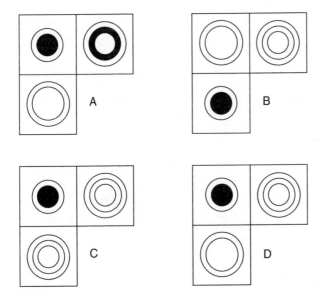

(viii)

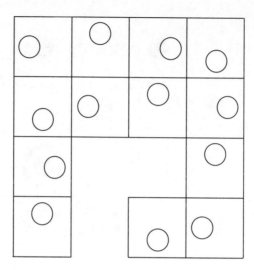

Which is the missing section?

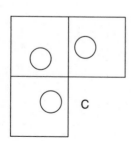

A

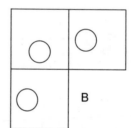

B

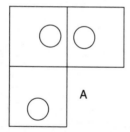

C

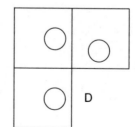

D

(ix)

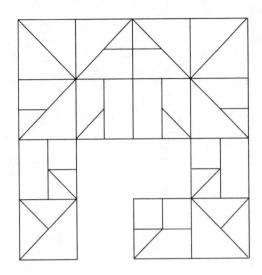

Which is the missing section?

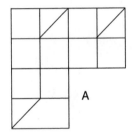

A

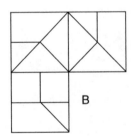

B

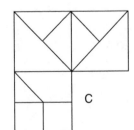

C

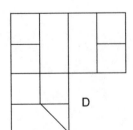

D

(x)

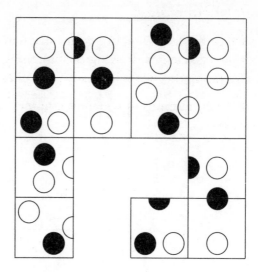

Which is the missing section?

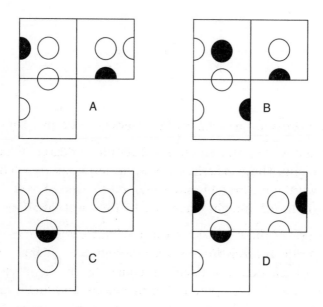

Symbolic interpretation

2   In each of the following use your imagination to create
    an original sketch or drawing of something recognizable
    incorporating the symbol already provided.

    You have 20 minutes in which to complete the six
    drawings.

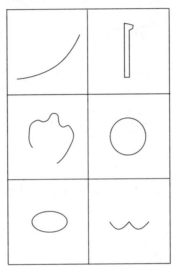

Lateral thinking word puzzles (Answers, see pp. 169–70)

3   All ten word puzzles in this test require a degree of lateral
    thinking. These exercises are not to test your knowledge
    of word meanings, but are designed to exercise your
    flexibility of thought when faced with novel situations.

    Several of these puzzles require what we sometimes
    describe as *three-dimensional thought*, i.e. an analysis of
    the puzzle before you, closer inspection of the puzzle to
    search for hidden patterns or meanings, and finally an
    exploration of the puzzle beyond its visible boundaries in
    your search for a solution.

There is no time limit with these puzzles. If you cannot solve them at the first attempt, do not be tempted to look straight at the answer. Instead return to the puzzle at a later time or date and have another look at the problem. It is possible that your subconscious mind has been analysing the puzzle all the while, and the answer may suddenly appear to you quickly and unexpectedly.

(i)   Carolina allspice

goose eggs

photo opportunities

bassoonists

the greenhouse effect

sea adders

What do the above have in common that the following do not?

bread and butter

traffic cops

(ii)   What letters should replace the question marks?

F	I
F	O

S	E
F	I

T	H
S	I

S	E
T	E

E	I
E	L

?	?
?	?

(iii) What word has been placed in the wrong column?

Column A Column B

faithful   broom

master   hand

soldier   born

fashioned moon

(iv)

archery

obvious

rocket

trident

symmetrical

rectify

hamburger

?

Which comes next?

accolade, biography, stealthily, acropolis or wickedest?

(v)

DAME	EDGE	ACRE	ROAD
RISE	AGOG	ROPE	EVEN
ARID	SPIN	INCH	AFAR
WIND	ELSE	APEX	**?**

What word should replace the question mark?

hope, rail, card, find, opus or that

(vi)   What do the following have in common?

the Common Market

peanuts

the Garden of Eden

plastic bags

fixed costs

(vii)   What letter should replace the question mark?

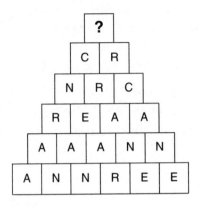

(viii) What do these words have in common?

herons, notes, toners, toothy

(ix)   Put these words into three groups of two words
each so that each pair of words has a common link.

tacit, wayfarer, elope, formal, governor, ruler

(x)   What feature do the following groups of letters
have in common?

LISS   NERK   WED   ZASS   EXD

The circles of your mind (Answer, see p. 171)

4   We observe symmetrical patterns every day of our lives as they occur in nature and in designs such as wallpaper or tiling. In this experiment we have created a circular symmetrical pattern of different designs of circles.

Following the ground rules already established, can you fill in all the remaining blank sections with the correct symbols to recreate the same symmetrical pattern?

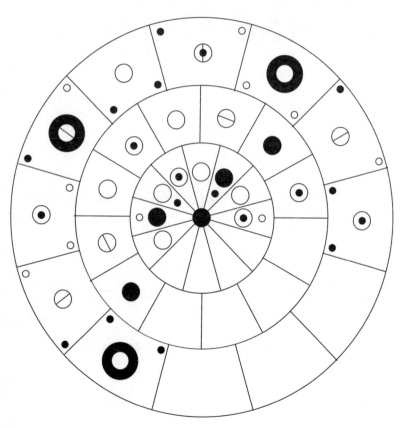

Divergent ability (Scoring/analysis, see p. 172)

5   This test is based on Gestalt and Jackson's Test of
    Divergent Ability, which requires the subject to name as
    many new uses as possible for everyday objects such as a
    brick or a piece of string.

    Here, you are required to name up to 12 new uses for a
    bucket in 10 minutes. You should work strictly to the
    time limit otherwise your score will be invalidated.

    1   ....

    2   ....

    3   ....

    4   ....

    5   ....

    6   ....

    7   ....

    8   ....

    9   ....

    10 ....

    11 ....

    12 ....

Rebuses (Answers, see pp. 172–3)

6   A rebus is the enigmatic representation in visual form of
    the sounds of a name or word. Rebus is a Latin word
    meaning *by things*, indicating a coded text which can be
    deciphered by studying its visual display.

    Four examples are shown below which illustrate the type
    of creative thinking necessary to solve such riddles.

    (i)   DES
           DES

    (ii)   : :
           : :
           : :
           : : : : :

    (iii) MEASU

    (iv)   M E
           A L

    Now try the following, the first set of six should produce
    just one word answers, while the second set of 12 each
    represent a familiar phrase.

    There is no time limit, we are simply aiming here to put
    your powers of creative thinking to the test. For any that
    you cannot solve we suggest you return to them later
    and have a fresh look. It is quite possible that the answer
    will suddenly come to you, as a result of your
    subconscious mind continuing to analyse the problem.

(v) One word

1. O_2H	2. B ⌒R⌒ A ⌒I⌒ N
3. (G HOG)	4. ETTE LA
5. NOMMAG	6. TPROUT

(vi) Familiar phrases

1. WORLⅭ	**2.** S I M D I Ⅽ I I I I L L	**3.** ...VOUS SYS...
4. WINDO SF	**5.** TO O	**6.** E N O K W G L D E
7. SE | SS IO | NS	**8.** TOGO BOARD	**9.** LOBSDUE
10. **THROUGH** THROUGH	**11.** FALL	**12.** CHIEF C N O S

The hidden star (Answer, see p. 174)

7 Find a perfect five-pointed star in the diagram below:

Lateral thinking number puzzles (Answers, see pp. 175–7)

8   This is a set of 10 number puzzles designed to exercise your powers of lateral thinking and creativity. None of these puzzles involve anything more than just a very basic knowledge of mathematics. What they do involve, however, is an ability not to take things at face value and to be able to think sideways and look beyond what appears before you on the paper. You must explore every possibility, for example, it might be necessary to study the numbers in relationship to the diagrams in which they are presented. Above all, be prepared for the unexpected, and allow your mind to search for the unlikely and unpredictable.

There is no time limit with these puzzles. If you cannot solve them at the first attempt, do not be tempted to look straight at the answer. Instead, return to the puzzle at a later time or date and have another look at the problem as it is possible that your subconscious mind has been analysing the puzzle all the while.

(i)   What number should replace the question mark?

4	7	1
6	1	3
4	2	3

5	1	3
2	8	5
2	3	1

1	2	6
2	1	2
4	5	?

(ii)   What number should replace the question mark?

21		22	20			
	22				21	21
	12			11		
		12			?	
21		22				21
	12			11		

(iii) Continue this sequence to its logical conclusion.

2	5	6	3	8	4

7	4	8	3	6

1	1	6	3	8

(iv)   What number should replace the question mark?

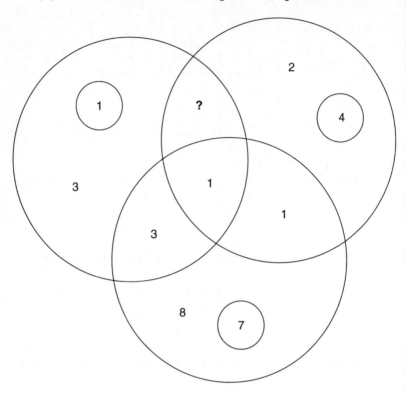

(v)   What numbers should replace the question marks?

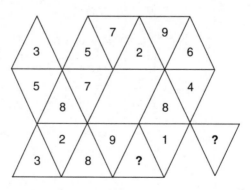

(vi)   What number should replace the question mark?

7	11	4	
12	2	?	9
15	3	3	18
	15	22	7

(vii)   What number should replace the question mark?

29	86	67	98
63			15
6			9
17	13	?	11

(viii) What numbers should replace the question marks?

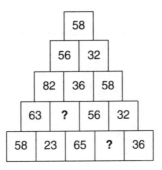

(ix)   What arrangement of dots should appear on the missing face?

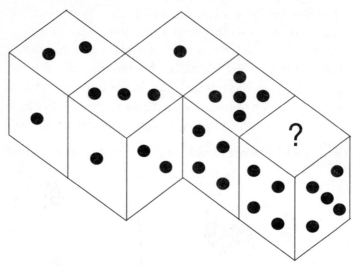

(x)   What number should replace the question mark?

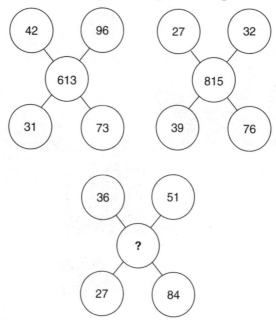

Interpretation

9 The object here is to interpret each of the twenty
drawings in the wildest and most imaginative way you
can. You may also try playing the game with other
people. The wilder you think someone's suggestion is,
the better it is and the more creative they are. For
example, you might think that drawing number 5 is a
pair of socks hanging from a washing line. But is there
anything else it can be? Let your imagination run riot
and see what you can come up with.

Situation puzzles (Answers, see pp. 177–8)

10 These real-life puzzles are designed to develop creative thought and problem-solving capacities. You have to use your imagination to try and arrive at an explanation for each scenario. A suggested answer is given in each case, but the main object is to come up with a plausible explanation.

Each of these situations can also be played as a game between two or more people. The situation is presented to the group, who must then try to find out what is going on by asking further questions. The person who initially presented the situation can only answer 'yes' or 'no' to questions (or occasionally 'irrelevant').

(i)   A man is running along a corridor with a piece of paper in his hand. The lights flicker and the man drops to his knees and cries out in despair.

(ii) A London workman visits eight foreign countries in one day, despite having no passport, and leaves of his own accord.

iii) Two men digging a trench suddenly looked at each other angrily and started to argue. They make a phone call to their boss after which one man goes home with a smile on his face and the other continues digging, angrier than ever.

iv)   Alan sat on Doris and killed her when the music stopped.

(v)   Harry regularly visits his grandfather on the 14th floor of an apartment building by going to the 12th floor and walking up two flights of stairs. Last year he only took the elevator to the 11th floor.

(vi) A couple go to a movie. During the movie the husband strangles his wife. He is able to get her body home without attracting attention.

(vii) A man tells his boss, 'I had a terrible dream last night that if you take your planned flight today, your plane will crash.' 'I should fire you', said the boss, 'but in view of your concern I will let you off with a warning.'

(viii) A lady enters a store and says 'Pain'. The shopkeeper gives her exactly what she requires.

(ix) At the bottom of my house is a straight road. I frequently drive east along this road for 300 yards, yet when I stop, my car is still facing east.

(x) A man is sitting on the window ledge of his twenty-storey apartment block. Suddenly he jumps off, but is not injured.

Sequential patterns (Answers, pp. 178–81)

11 In each of the following decide what pattern or movement is occurring, then draw what you consider to be the missing figure to complete the pattern or sequence.

You have 45 minutes to complete the ten questions.

(i)

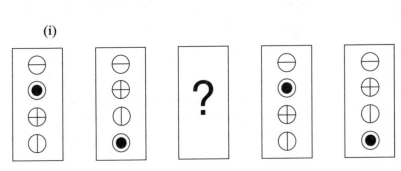

(ii)

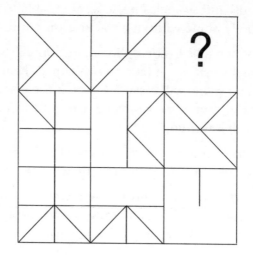

(iii)

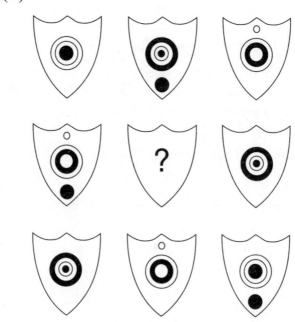

(iv)

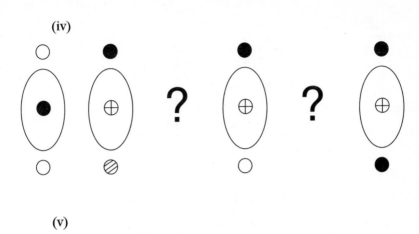

(v)

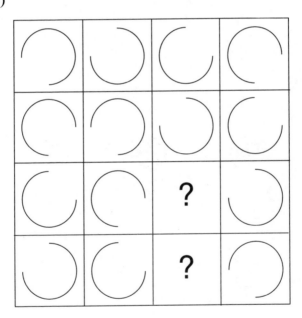

(vi)

(vii)

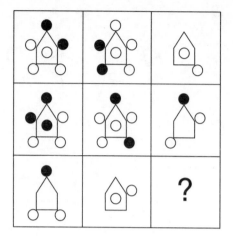

(viii)

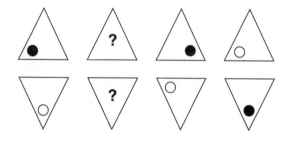

(ix)

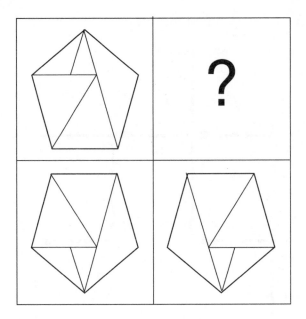

(x)

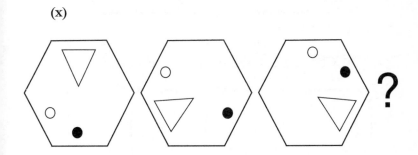

Matchstick puzzles (Answers, see pp. 182–84)

12   (i)   Change 3 matches to create 3 squares.

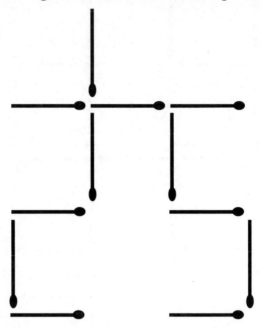

(ii)   Change 2 matches to create 4 squares.

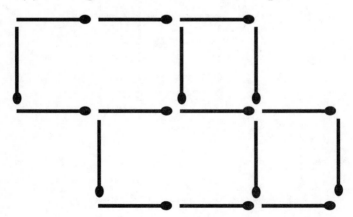

(iii) Change 3 matches to create 5 squares.

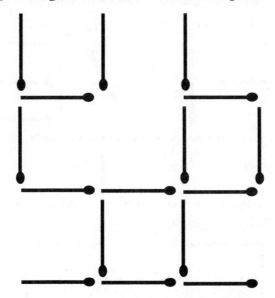

(iv) Change 3 matches to create 4 squares.

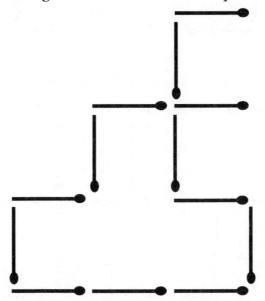

(v)   First arrange 10 matches to equal 5.

Then take away 7 matches and leave 4.

(vi)   Re-arrange 3 six-pointed stars to form one large six-pointed star.

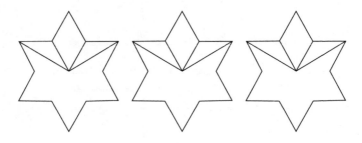

2

Problem solving

In psychology a problem is defined as a situation in which some of the components are already known and additional components must then be ascertained or determined. Such situations are of interest to psychologists when these unknown factors are neither obvious, nor easily ascertained.

Problem solving is broadly all the processes involved in the solution of a problem, and in psychology is the area of cognitive psychology that is concerned with these processes. Examples of classic puzzles used by psychologists as exercises in problem solving are anagrams, puzzle boxes and water-jug problems.

The following is a typical example of the type of puzzle which concerns itself with the process of problem solving:

How is it possible to measure 9 minutes when you have only a 4-minute sand glass and a 7-minute sand glass?

Solution:

Start both glasses running at the same time. Turn the 4-minute glass over as soon as it runs out (4 minutes). Then turn the 7-minute glass over when it runs out (an extra 3 minutes). At that moment, the 4-minute glass has 1 minute left. Turn it over when that 1 minute is

over (plus 1 minute). Then turn the 7-minute glass
over, which ran for only 1 minute (plus 1 minute). That
makes a total of 9 minutes (4 + 3 + 1 + 1).

Of course, real-life problems are a somewhat different
proposition but the thought processes necessary in tackling
them are the same as those involved in the analysis, and
finding of solutions, of problems, or puzzles, that are
artificially set.

The subtle difference between puzzles and problems is
that a puzzle is set by another person, and has a solution
already known to that person. A problem, on the other
hand, arises in life. It is not set artificially and there is not an
answer already known to someone else. There is no right
answer but some solutions are likely to be better than
others.

One of the key points to bear in mind when tackling a
real-life problem is not to spend too much time complaining
about the problem or falling into the trap of wallowing in
self-pity. Instead of this it is much better to talk *at* the
problem and not about it. Admittedly, for many serious
personal problems this is much easier said than done, but in
almost all cases a positive approach is much better than a
negative one.

With many problems or difficult situations it is essential to
get to the heart of the problem. In one of the opening lines
of the 1946 movie of Raymond Chandler's *The Big Sleep*,
Humphrey Bogart, as Philip Marlowe, remarks, 'Get Mr Big
and you get them all.' This is true of many problems, where
if you get right to the heart of the problem and can find a
solution to the main cause, then it is amazing how quickly
all the peripheral problems also disappear.

There are many different problem-solving techniques that
have been put into practice over the years. Perhaps the best

known of these is *brainstorming* which is a group problem-solving technique in which all the participants are encouraged to let fly with ideas and possible solutions to the problem in hand.

Brainstorming is, therefore, a method of searching for, and developing creative solutions to a problem by focusing on the problem and deliberately encouraging the participants to come up with as many unusual solutions as possible. During such sessions there should be no criticism of ideas as the aim is to introduce as many different ideas as possible, and to break down any preconceptions about limits of the problem. Then, once this has been done, the results and ideas can be analysed and the best proposed solutions further explored.

Participants in such brainstorming sessions need not necessarily be experts in the field under scrutiny, nor should they necessarily be already aware of the problem under consideration. They should ideally come from as wide a range of disciplines and backgrounds as possible. This brings many more creative ideas to the session, and often someone looking at a problem from the outside may suddenly come up with a possible solution that someone heavily involved on the inside has not considered.

Although it is generally not as effective as a group session, brainstorming can also be carried out individually. While such individual brainstorming can sometimes produce a wider range of ideas than a group session, these ideas tend not to be developed as effectively because individually it is more difficult to tackle and solve any additional problems that may be encountered. On the other hand, individuals are free to explore their ideas in their own time without being pressurized by other group members and without fear of criticism.

One of the great benefits of individual brainstorming is that it is a method of attacking a problem and encouraging your brain to function in a creative and positive way by exploring new ideas and solutions.

Another tried and tested method of problem solving is *Critical Path Analysis*. As a mind tool this is an effective method of analysing a complex problem or project, and it is a particularly useful tool where there is a time factor or deadline involved.

The concept behind critical path analysis is the need to formulate a plan of action because some activities are dependent on other activities being completed first. For example, you cannot convert your garage into a living room unless you have drawn up plans, obtained pricing estimates and, in some cases, obtained planning permission. Such dependent activities need, therefore, to be completed in sequence, with each activity usually completed, or nearly completed, before the next activity can begin.

A third problem-solving technique is known as *SWOT Analysis* – **S**trengths, **W**eaknesses, **O**pportunities, **T**hreats. This technique can be an effective method of identifying your strengths and weaknesses and of examining the opportunities and threats faced.

In order to carry out a SWOT analysis, start by writing down answers to the following questions:

Strengths

What are your strengths?
What are you good at?

These questions should be considered both from your own point of view and from the point of view of others you deal with. At all times you must be honest and realistic with yourself and able to recognize many of your own characteristics, many of which could turn out to be your strengths.

Weaknesses

In what ways can you improve?
What do you do badly?
What should you avoid doing?

Again, you must be realistic for the exercise to be effective, and again you should answer not just from your own point of view, but from the point of view of others.

Opportunities

What opportunities, immediate or otherwise, would
   be good for you?
What would be most interesting to you?

Anything relevant, or possibly relevant should be considered, for example, changes in technology, lifestyle changes, career advancement.

Threats

What obstacles do you face?
What financial constraints exist?
What specifications must I adhere to?

Whether the problem, or task, is a small or a large one, the carrying out of such an analysis can be an illuminating one, not just in identifying what needs to be done, but in putting any problems into perspective and helping to identify your own strengths, which can then be built upon, and your own weaknesses, which can then be worked upon.

In the remainder of this chapter we present a collection of 25 general brainteasers which involve different kinds of thought processes, followed by a collection of 20 numerical brainteasers, also involving a variety of different types of approaches. For the more difficult puzzles, hints are provided and full detailed explanations are provided with the answers.

While both puzzles and problems bring their rewards, some people may prefer one to the other. Certainly, the successful solution of a problem achieves a worthwhile goal, and perhaps the major benefit to be obtained from tackling puzzles is that they stretch and exercise the mind and enable you to tackle the problems of real life with renewed vigour and confidence.

Before tackling the following selection of puzzles it may help you to consider the following four brainteasers as examples of the thought processes necessary to solve such puzzles.

Example 1

There are several versions of counterfeit coin puzzles where it is necessary to find the counterfeit coin, or coins, from a number of weighings. Most of these puzzles assume you have balance type scales available with two pans, where one object can be weighed against another. In this puzzle you have a single scale only with just one pan, which will weigh just one object, or group of objects at a time. You have three bags with an unspecified number of coins in each bag. One of the bags consists entirely of counterfeit coins weighing 75 grams each; the genuine coins weigh 70 grams each.

What is the minimum number of weighing operations you need to carry out before you can be certain of identifying the bag of counterfeit coins?

Solution:

Only one weighing operation.

Explanation:

Take one coin from bag 1, two coins from bag 2 and three coins from bag 3. Weigh all six coins together. If they weigh 425g, the first bag contains the counterfeit coin (1 coin at 75g + 5 coins at 70g = 425), if they weigh 430g, it is the second bag, and if they weigh 435g, it is the third bag.

Example 2

A company gives a choice of two plans to the union negotiator for an annual increase in salary.

First option: Initial salary £20000 to be increased after each 12 months by £500.

Second option: Initial salary £20000 to be increased after each six months by £125.

The salary is to be calculated every 6 months. Which plan should the union negotiator recommend to his members?

Solution:

The second plan.

Explanation:

At first glance it appears obvious that the union negotiator should recommend the first option as this will give £500 increase per year and the second will only give £250 increase per year. However, this is not the case. Let us examine the two options more closely:

First option   (£500 increase after each 12 months):

First year	£10000 + £10000 = £20000
Second year	£10250 + £10250 = £20500

Second option (£125 increase after each 6 months):

> First year   £10000 + £10125 = £20125
> Second year   £10250 + £10375 = £20625

So the second plan should be accepted.

Example 3

Two identical bags each contain 8 counters, 4 white and 4 black. One counter is drawn out of bag one and another counter out of bag two. What are the chances that at least one of the balls will be black?

Answer:

Three chances in four.

Explanation:

Look at the possible combinations of drawing a counter from each bag. These are:

> a.   black – black
> b.   white – white
> c.   black – white
> d.   white – black

Out of these four possible combinations there is only one, the white – white combination, where black does not occur. The chances, therefore, of drawing at least one black ball are three chances in four.

Example 4

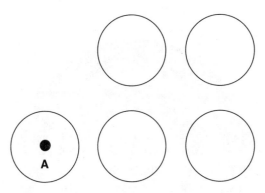

All five circles have the same diameter. Draw a line passing
through point A in such a way that it divides the five circles
into two equal areas.

Answer:

By drawing three additional imaginary circles to create a
symmetrical block of eight circles, the problem is
considerably simplified and leads to the following solution:

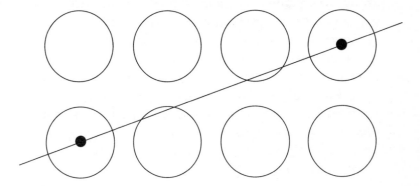

The puzzles (Answers, see pp. 185–92)

1

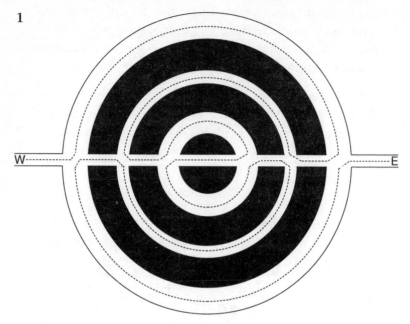

A man walks through a park from West to East but decides he needs to take some extra exercise by walking around every one of the park's three circular paths instead of just walking along the main central drive, for example, the dotted line shows one particular route which he can take to achieve this objective. However, how many different routes are there by which he is able to do this? He does not go over any part of the route twice but does, inevitably, arrive at the same point more than once on his travels.

(Hint, see p. 160)

2   In the game of draughts a piece (draughtsman) can jump
    over another piece in any direction, including diagonally.
    A draughtsman is removed when another piece jumps
    over it. In one move you can make your piece jump over
    a series of other pieces.

    Make just one move so that only eight pieces remain on
    the board, so arranged that no horizontal, vertical or
    corner to corner line contains more than one piece.

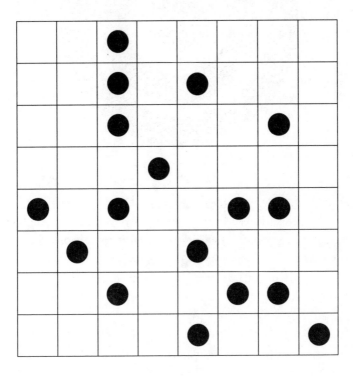

3

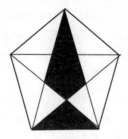

What is the ratio between the two shaded areas in the diagram above? (Hint, see p. 160)

4

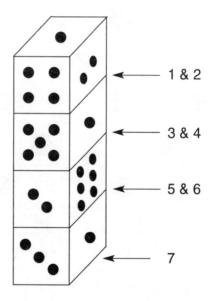

Without looking at a real die, can you quickly calculate the total of spots on faces 1, 2, 3, 4, 5, 6 and 7?
(Hint, see p. 160)

5   'I want to hold a dinner party,' said my wife, 'but I want to invite only a very few guests.'

'OK,' I said, 'then as well as the two of us, I suggest you invite your sister Jane, her brother-in-law and his wife, my son Keith, my book editor Alex and her husband and son, and Mrs Morgan, the widow from next door, and her nephew who I happen to know is visiting her tomorrow.'

'That sounds to be more than I was intending to invite,' said my wife. 'No it isn't,' was my reply, 'It is actually very few people, just think about it.'

How many were at the dinner party? (Hint, see p. 160)

6   A ball is put in an empty bag. You do not know whether the ball is black or white. A second ball which you know to be white is then put in the bag. A ball is then drawn out, and it proves to be white.

What are the chances that the ball remaining in the bag is also white?

7   I was on the third floor of a department store recently with my wife and we decided to take the lift to the top floor. When we pushed the button the lift was already on the 7th floor, after which it went up to the 9th floor, down to the 6th, back up to the 11th and down to the 4th.

'This is hopeless,' I said, 'we may as well walk.' 'No,' said my wife, 'just be patient, the lift will now go up to the 12th floor, then it will come back to us at last, however, it will then take us up to a certain floor whether we like it or not.'

How did my wife know that it would visit us after the 12th floor, and which floor would it then take us to, whether we liked it or not? (Hint, see p. 161)

8

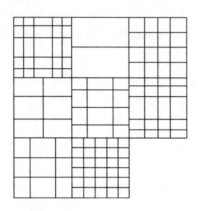

Which is the missing square?

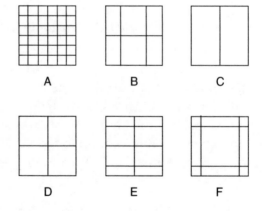

A   B   C

D   E   F

(Hint, see p. 161)

9   68932, 71456, 98372, 14568

What comes next?

    56381, 89372, 29347, 82943 or 75286?

(Hint, see p. 161)

10 Heathcliffe sent Cathy the cryptic message below. What does it mean?

    beseech

    lament

    Cathy

    footworn

    abyss

    wither

    Heathcliffe

(Hint, see p. 161)

11

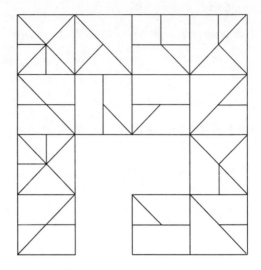

Which is the missing section?

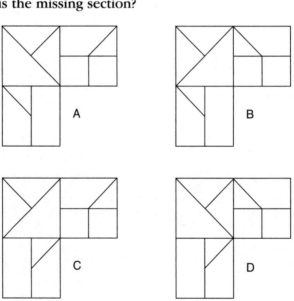

(Hint, see p. 161)

12

Arrange the digits 1–9 in the circles in such a way that:

Numbers 1 and 2 and all the digits between them add up to 9.

Numbers 2 and 3 and all the digits between them add up to 19.

Numbers 3 and 4 and all the digits between them add up to 45.

Numbers 4 and 5 and all the digits between them add up to 18.

(Hint, see p. 161)

13   In a bag of apples, 4 out of 50 contain a worm. What are the chances of picking out just 3 apples and finding they all contain a worm? (Hint, see p. 161)

14   Can you draw the missing arrangement of dots?

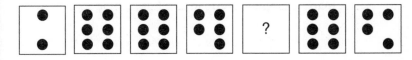

(Hint, see p. 161)

15

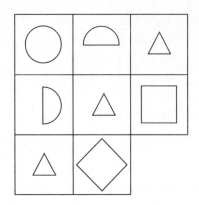

Which is the missing square? (Hint, see p. 161)

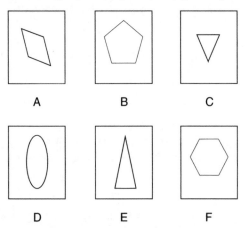

A   B   C

D   E   F

16   How many triangles occur in the figure below?

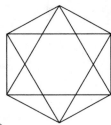

Hint, see p. 161)

17   The game of pool or snooker calls for a high degree of
     skill and concentration, coupled with a great deal of
     creative thinking. In this example you have just one ball,
     the black ball, on the table and you need to pocket it with
     the white ball. Several of your opponent's balls, the
     striped balls, are on the table and you must figure out
     how to shoot your last remaining ball into a pocket
     without touching any of the striped balls in the process.
     Work out how you can strike the white ball to travel round
     the table and knock the black ball into a pocket by
     rebounding off the minimum number of sides of the table.

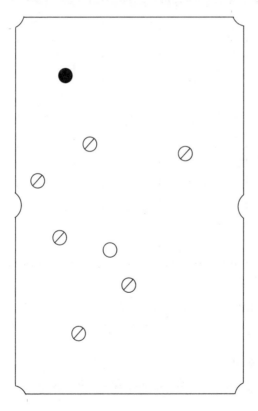

(Hint, see p. 162)

18   I did the City of Leeds half-marathon recently. However, after I had completed the first two-thirds of the course I developed a blister on my foot and had to hobble the rest of the way to the finishing line. It took me just twice as long to hobble the remainder of the race as it did to run the first two thirds.

How many times faster did I run than I hobbled?

(Hint, see p. 162)

19   What number should replace the question mark?

```
            4       3
        5       2       3
     6       1       4       2
     3       5       1       4
        2       1       ?
            2       5
```

(Hint, see p. 162)

20   point + pivot = cavity

advice + drivel = taxes

knives + knife = sever

Therefore:

review + envoi = ?

Choose from:

Bahrain, China, Brazil, Mexico, Latvia

(Hint, see p. 162)

21 If we presented you with the words MAR, AM and FAR and asked you to find the smallest word that contained all the letters from which these words could be produced, we would expect you to come up with the word FARM.

Here is a further list of words:

DAMSEL, LEASH, MELODY, LEMON

What is the shortest English word from which all these four words can be produced? (Hint, see p. 162)

22 Which group of letters is the odd one out?

LNQP   JLNM   DFIH
GILK   SUXW

(Hint, see p. 162)

23 Paul has 26 cards each featuring a different letter of the alphabet which he places face down on the table and then turns over at random one by one.

What are the odds that the first four cards to be turned over will spell out his name P_A_U_L in the correct order, and what are the chances that the last four cards, instead of the first four cards, will spell out P_A_U_L in the correct order? (Hint, see p. 162)

24 What message is concealed in the array of words below?

milk	arch	kind	echo
able	pond	star	show
idea	monk	hide	host
plum	pure	vote	left

(Hint, see p. 162)

25 What arrangements of dots should replace the question
   marks? (Hint, see p. 162)

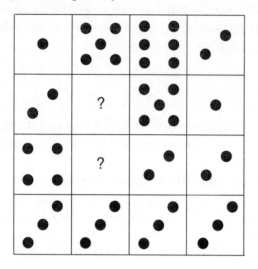

Numerical problem solving
(Answers, see pp. 193–202)

Mathematics may be defined as the subject we
never know what we are talking about, nor
whether what we are saying is true.

Bertrand Russell

Problems involving the use of mathematics can be
challenging, fascinating, confusing and frustrating, but once
you have developed an interest in numbers, a whole new
world is opened up as you discover their many
characteristics and patterns.

We all require some numerical skills in our lives, whether
it is to calculate our weekly shopping bill or to budget how
to use our monthly income, however, for many people
mathematics is a subject they consider to be too difficult
when confronted by what are considered to be its higher

branches. When broken down and analysed, and explained in layman's terms, however, many of these aspects can be readily understood by those of us with only a rudimentary grasp of the subject.

The following section consists of a set of 20 difficult numerical problems which involve several kinds of calculation, reasoning and logic. The more you practise on this type of puzzle, the more you will come to understand the thought processes and analysis necessary to solve them and the more proficient you will become at arriving at the correct solution.

Hints are provided for the most difficult puzzles and in all cases we provide full detailed explanations as to how you should tackle the problem to arrive at the correct solution.

1   If a half of 5 were 3, what would one-third of 10 be?

2   Jimmy has 10 pockets and 44 coins. Each coin value = 1 Euro.

    He wants to place the 44 coins into his 10 pockets so that each pocket contains a different number of coins.

    Can he do this?

3   At a college 100 students were studying languages.

27 students studied	Latin
49 students studied	French
35 students studied	German
8 students studied	Latin/French
6 students studied	Latin/German
9 students studied	French/German
3 students studied	Latin/French/German

How many students studied none of the 3 languages?

(Hints for puzzles 1, 2, 3, see p. 163)

4   Two golfers, Geoff and Harry, decided to have a wager on the golf course. They intended to play 18 holes and have a wager on each hole. Geoff said to Harry, 'We will wager on each hole, half of the money in my wallet. I have £100 in my wallet.'

After playing 12 holes it began to rain so they retired to the club house. As Geoff had won 6 holes, Harry had won 4 holes and 2 holes were tied, Geoff said, 'I will buy the drinks.' However, looking in his wallet he found that he had lost £28. How did that happen?

5   In a room that is full of aliens from another planet:

1   There is more than one alien.
2   Each alien has the same number of fingers.
3   Each alien has at least one finger on each of his hands.
4   In the room the total number of fingers lies between 200 and 300.
5   If you knew the total number of fingers in the room, you would know how many aliens there were.

How many aliens were there?

How many fingers did each alien have?

(Hints for puzzles 4, 5, see p. 163)

6 I wanted to know the month when the circus was
   coming to town, so I asked six of my friends. These were
   their answers:

   Alan said: 'It begins with the letter J.'
   Barbara said: 'It has only 5 letters in its name.'
   Carol said: 'It has 30 days in its month.'
   David said: 'It has 31 days in its month.'
   Edward said: 'It has 3 vowels in its month.'
   Fiona said: 'It ends in Y.'

   But half had lied.

   Which month was it?

7 A bookmaker was lying odds on a race:

   SANDS OF TIME   2–1 Against
   LITTLE BEN   3–1 Against
   MOONSHINE   4–1 Against
   PHIL'S FOLLY   8–5 Against
   ABANDON ALL HOPE   10–1 Against
   CATCH KEN   ?

   CATCH KEN has no odds yet decided. What odds should
   the bookmaker offer to give himself a margin on 15%,
   assuming that he is able to balance his books?

   (Hints for puzzles 6, 7, see p. 164)

8   An old fairground game consisted of a sheet of linoleum which had a pattern of 4" squares drawn on it.

   If the player threw a 2½" diameter coin on it, what are the chances that the coin will fall not touching a line? (Hint, see p. 164)

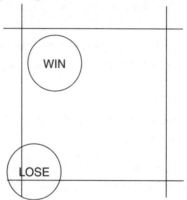

9   What number should replace the question mark? (Hint, see p. 165)

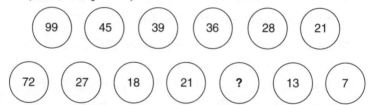

| 99 | 45 | 39 | 36 | 28 | 21 |

| 72 | 27 | 18 | 21 | ? | 13 | 7 |

10   How many revolutions must the large cog make to return all the cogs to their starting positions? (Hint, see p. 165)

11   When the Rajah died he left a box containing a collection of diamonds.

To his eldest son he left one diamond, to the eldest son's wife he left one-ninth of those remaining.

To his second son he left 2 diamonds, to the second son's wife he left one-ninth of those remaining.

To his third son he left 3 diamonds, to the third son's wife he left one ninth of those remaining.

And so on.

The wife of the youngest son found that there were no diamonds left for her.

How many diamonds did the Rajah have, and how many sons did he have?

12   There is a bamboo cane 10 feet high, the upper end of which has been broken down and now reaches the ground, its tip lying just 3 feet from the stem.

What is the height of the break from the ground?

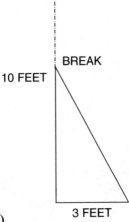

10 FEET

BREAK

3 FEET

(Hint, see p. 165)

13

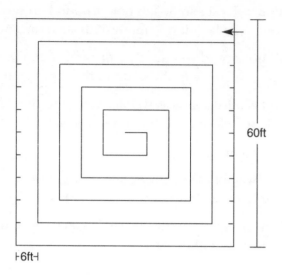

Starting at the top right-hand corner and spiralling inwards, how far would you have to travel to arrive at the centre? (Hint, see p. 166)

14 The state of Cattattackya was overrun with mice, so the King decreed that all the cats should exterminate the vermin.

At the end of the year the dead mice were counted and the total was 1,111,111, each cat had killed an equal number of mice.

Less than 500 cats achieved this remarkable feat.

How many cats were there in Cattattackya?

(Hint, see p. 166)

15   Jim is trying to find out where Tim lives. He knows that the numbers in his road are 8 to 100 inclusive.

Jim asks, 'Is it greater than 50?' and Tim answers and lies.

Then Jim asks, 'Is the number a multiple of 4?' and Tim answers and again lies.

Then Jim asks, 'Is it a perfect square?' and Tim answers and this time he tells the truth.

Then Jim asks, 'Is the first digit 3?' and Tim replies (truthfully or not).

Jim tells him his number but he is wrong.

What is the number?

16   A woman had seven children. On multiplying their ages together one obtains the number 6591.

Given that today is the birthday of all seven, how many triplets are there and what are all seven ages?

17   $\sqrt{5}$ is irrational. Its decimal goes on to infinity. To 6 decimal places it is 2.236068.

Find the value of:

$\dfrac{3}{\sqrt{5}}$ by a simple calculation.

18   $[3 (230 + t)^2 = 492?04$

Find which digit replaces the question mark.

19   What are the true odds against winning the lottery of 49 numbers?

(Hint for puzzles 15–19, see p. 166)

20   The carpet in a room was coloured as follows: $\frac{1}{3}$ is black, $\frac{1}{4}$ is red, and the remainder is yellow measuring 8 square yards.

What is the total area of the room?

3

Memory

Memory is the process of storing and retrieving information in the brain. It is this process of memory that is central to learning and thinking. Human beings are continually learning throughout their lifetime. Only some of this massive volume of information is selected and stored and thus becomes available for recalling later when required. Learning is the acquisition of new knowledge, and memory is the retention of this knowledge. The combination of learning and memory, therefore, is the basis of all our knowledge and abilities and is what enables us to consider the past, exist in the present and plan for the future.

Four different types of remembering are distinguished by psychologists: recollection, recall, recognition and relearning.

It is established that there are two main categories of memory: *declarative* memory, and *procedural* memory. Declarative memory is all we have experienced in the form of information gained from childhood onwards and is the memory for facts and events, such as remembering, for example, birthdays, telephone numbers and historical facts.

Procedural memory is the memory for procedures and abilities and it stores information which enables us, for example, to drive a car, tie our shoe laces or play a musical instrument.

The memory for historical and other events, our declarative memory, may be easier to build up, but is easily lost or forgotten, whereas our memory for skills learning might require a repetitive practice (relearning), in fact, is likely to considerably improve with practice and experience – *practice makes perfect*.

While little is known about the physiology of memory storage in the brain, what is known is that memory is not situated in only one part of the brain, but involves the association of several brain systems working together.

The temporal lobe, which is located under the temporal bone above the ears is thought to be particularly important for the storage of past events and includes the temporal neocortex which is thought to be potentially the region involved in long-term memory. This region also contains a group of interconnected structures that appear to perform the declarative memory function. Studies suggest that one of these circuits through the hippocampus and thalamus may be involved in spatial memories, whereas another circuit through the amygdala and thalmus, may be responsible for our emotional memories.

Memory can be broadly divided into three types: *sensory* (immediate) memory, *working* (short-term) memory and *long-term* memory.

Sensory, or immediate memory, is of all present occurrences such as noises and events that are seen as pictures in your mind. A sensory memory exists for different types of stimuli received through the senses. These are iconic memory for visual stimuli, echoic memory for aural stimuli and haptic memory for touch. The sensory memory filters all the different stimuli received at a given instant in time and only passes to short-term memory what is of interest.

Working, or short-term, memory enables the brain to evaluate the mass of incoming stimuli, or information and select what is to be retained and memorized and what is to be rejected. It is this part of the memory which enables us to temporarily recall any information currently under process, for example, if someone is speaking to you, it is only possible to understand them if you can recall what they said when they started speaking.

Because working memory decays rapidly, it only has a limited capacity. There are ways in which short-term memory can be improved. One of these techniques is known as chunking, for example, this is why a hyphenated telephone number is easier to memorize than a single long number, and this technique can lead to an increase, albeit temporarily, in short-term memory capacity.

A hindrance to short-term memory, which all of us will have experienced many times, is interference. This is when your train of thought is interrupted, thus causing a disturbance in short-term memory retention. It is, therefore, desirable to complete tasks involving short-term memory as quickly as possible and without interruption.

Long-term memory is intended for the storage of information over a long period and involves things like telephone numbers, holiday plans, names and addresses, and memories evoked from the past. Information from the working memory is transferred to long-term memory after a few seconds and, unlike working memory, there is little decay.

Long-term memory is split into two sub-divisions: episodic memory and semantic memory. Episodic memory is our memory of events and experiences from which we can recall and reconstruct actual events that took place at a given point in our lifetime. Semantic memory, on the other hand, is the structured record of facts and skills which we have acquired during our lifetime.

The three main functions of long-term memory are storage, deletion and retrieval. Once a piece of information has been passed to long-term memory from working memory it is stored until it needs to be retrieved. Deletion is mainly caused by decay and interference, although it is argued that, once stored, a piece of information is in our long-term memory forever, however, it may become increasingly difficult to access certain items, and this is why much information may be recalled only with prompting.

There are certain techniques by which we are all able to improve our memory. While very little is yet known about the mechanics of memory, it is accepted that the more you use it the better it becomes. It is also accepted that while it is impossible to improve on past memories, it is possible to improve one's memory for the present and future by practising active recall during learning, by periodic reviews of the material, and by overlearning the material beyond the point of mastery. In addition, there is the technique of mnemonics, which involves the use of association, imagination and location to remember particular facts.

It is, therefore, important to stimulate the memory by using it to the utmost, continually accepting different challenges and learning new skills. In addition to the enriching of our lives this could also stimulate our brain's neural circuits to grow and strengthen.

The tests which follow are not only designed to test your powers of memory but to assist you in improving your memory by developing your powers of concentration and to discipline yourself to fix your mind on the subject being studied.

Memory tests

1   P   K   L   I   A   N   Y   D

Study the above letters for 60 seconds then turn to page 89.

2   Study the grid below for 2 minutes then turn to pages 89 and 90.

			3					
		3	4	7	3	2		
			7		1			
			3	2	9	4		
	3	1	2			7		
						2		
						1		

3   This exercise tests your ability to remember pairs of
    words as they are shown in the pairing below.

CAMERA	SNOWMAN	HAND
RAFT	CLOCK	ELEPHANT
CHAIN	WHEEL	TRAMPOLINE
MOUSE	HAYSTACK	RICKSHAW
CHURCH	TOWEL	TELEPHONE
BEACH	WALLPAPER	ALSATIAN
ZIPPER	CHIMNEY	BRUSH
YACHT	HOTEL	RIVER

Study the 12 pairs of words for 15 minutes and then link
each pair.

Now turn to pages 90 and 91.

4   Study the following pairs of letters for 30 seconds then
    turn to page 91.

    ED   CA   BE   TI   NE

5   Here is a further exercise similar to exercise 3.

AQUARIUM	SWAMP	DRAGON
STETHOSCOPE	TANDEM	UNIVERSITY
JACKET	ROOF	LION
BICYCLE	KNOT	PROJECT

MUSHROOM	DIAMOND	WALK
TRUMPET	NEPTUNE	TANK
SPAIN	LETTUCE	TRANSMIT
RUGBY	BADGE	REPUBLIC

As in exercise 3, this exercise tests your ability to remember pairs of words and form associations. Study the 12 pairs of words for 15 minutes and link each pair of words in your memory.

Now turn to page 92.

6 Study the word grid below for 3 minutes then turn to pages 93 and 94.

¹C	²A	³R	⁴A	⁵P
⁶A	R	A	B	A
⁷B	O	B	A	C
⁸A	B	A	T	E
⁹S	A	T	E	D

7

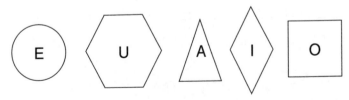

Study the above for 2 minutes then turn to page 94.

8   Study the following number grid for 60 seconds.

7	7	7	3	6	6	6	6
7	7	7	3	3	6	1	6
7	9	9	9	3	1	1	6
7	9	2	9	8	1	1	6
4	4	2	9	8	5	5	5
4	4	2	2	8	8	5	8
4	4	2	2	2	8	5	8
4	4	4	4	2	8	8	8

Now turn to page 94.

9   Study these number plates for 60 seconds then turn to page 95.

F389CK

T156LN

B724MS

10 Study the following faces for 3 minutes then turn to page 96.

11   Study the following for 3 minutes then turn to page 96.

12   Study the following for 30 seconds then turn to page 97.

13   Study the following for 3 minutes then turn to page 97.

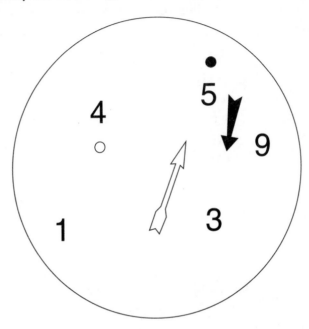

14   Study the following for 3 minutes then turn to page 98.

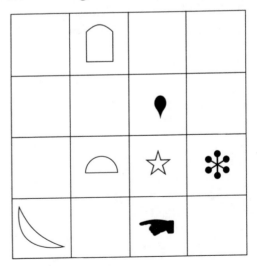

15   Attempt to memorize as many of these 48 words as you can in 5 minutes, then turn to page 98 and answer the questions.

TREES	MUSICAL INSTRUMENTS	REPTILES	BOATS
CALABASH	FIDDLE	TURTLE	CARVEL
ROWAN	CORNET	COBRA	BARQUE
WALNUT	GUITAR	GECKO	TRAWLER
HAZEL	BAGPIPES	VIPER	FELUCCA
ELM	UKELELE	SERPENT	PONTOON
POPLAR	VIOLIN	TADPOLE	STEAMER

VEHICLES	DOGS	PLANTS	COUNTRIES
OMNIBUS	BULLDOG	JASMINE`	PANAMA
SCOOTER	LURCHER	IRIS	AUSTRALIA
FLIVVER	DACHSHUND	ACANTHUS	GREECE
TAXICAB	TERRIER	HEATHER	POLAND
MINIBUS	SHEEPDOG	BEGONIA	LATVIA
AMBULANCE	HUSKY	MIMOSA	RUSSIA

16   Study the meanings of these 21 boys' names for 10 minutes. Then turn to page 99 and answer as many of the questions as you can.

ADAM – Redness
BRIAN – Hill
CRAIG – Rock
DAVID – Friend
EDWARD – Guardian
FRED – Ruler
GEOFFREY – Peace
HAROLD – Army
JOHN – Jehova
KENNETH – Fair

LESLIE – Scottish place
MARTIN – Mars
NEIL – Champion
PETER – Stone
ROBERT – Fame
STEPHEN – Crown
STUART – Steward
THOMAS – Twin
VINCENT – Conquer
WALTER – Ruler

Questions

1   (i)   What word is spelled out by the 2nd, 4th, 6th and 8th letters?

(ii)   What letter is two to the left of the letter A?

(iii) What letter is immediately to the right of the letter N?

(iv)   What word is spelled out by the 1st, 3rd, 5th and 7th letters?

(v)   What word is spelled out by reversing the order of the middle 4 letters?

2   (i)   Which of these numbers appears in a line reading downwards?

5219, 4721, 3842, 7321, 2472

(ii) Which of these numbers is repeated both horizontally and vertically?

21221, 31972, 32473, 34732, 23194

iii) Fill in the missing digit to complete one of the numbers reading across:

3–94

iv) Which of these numbers appears in a line reading downwards?

319, 312, 219, 329, 712

(v) Which of these numbers appears in a line reading across?

213, 132, 321, 312, 231

3

RICKSHAW ....

TOWEL ....

CAMERA ....

RIVER ....

BRUSH.....................................

ZIPPER.....................................

MOUSE ....

ELEPHANT..............................

RAFT ....

HAND ....

TELEPHONE ....

SNOWMAN ....

CHURCH ....

BEACH ....

CHAIN ....

CHIMNEY ....

YACHT ....

HAYSTACK ....

TRAMPOLINE ....

CLOCK ....

WHEEL ....

HOTEL.......................................

ALSATIAN ....

WALLPAPER ....

Put a letter A against one pair, the letter B against a second pair, etc., through to the letter L until you have matched what you think are the original 12 pairs of words.

4   (i)   Which three words below can be produced by combining two pairs of letters from the list?

   CANE   TIDE   ABET   NEED

   CARE   BEAD   TIED   EDIT

   (ii)   Which is the only pair of letters in the original list that has not been used in the three words that you have selected?

5   UNIVERSITY ....

LION ....

AQUARIUM ....

TRUMPET ....

TANK ....

JACKET ....

BICYCLE ....

RUGBY ....

TRANSMIT ....

DRAGON ....

KNOT ....

MUSHROOM ....

REPUBLIC ....

STETHOSCOPE ....

ROOF ....

SPAIN ....

LETTUCE ....

NEPTUNE ....

TANDEM ....

SWAMP ....

BADGE ....

WALK ....

DIAMOND ....

PROJECT ....

Put a letter A against one pair, the letter B against a second pair, etc., through to the letter L until you have matched what you think are the original 12 pairs of words.

6 (i)   Which of these words appears in a line reading across?

COPAC, SORAC, BOBAC, POPAC, BABAC

(ii) Which is the only word to appear both in a line reading across and a line reading down?

(iii) The name of which African capital city appears in a line reading downwards?

(iv) Complete the following word which appears in a line reading across:

– – T – D

(v)   Which of the following words appears in a line reading downwards?

ABORA, ADOBE, ACORA, AROBA, AROMA

(vi) What word appears in the end column reading downwards?

(vii) Which of these words appears in a line reading across?

CARAT, CAROB, CARAP, CAPER, CORAB

(viii) Which of these words appears in a line reading across?

ABARO, ABARA, ARABO, ARORA, ARABA

(ix) Which of these words appears in a line reading downwards?

CABAS, CABOS, TAPAS, TABAS, COBAS

(x) Based on your choices above, how accurately can you reconstruct the original word grid?

7 (i) What shape contains the letter A?

(ii) What letter is inside the square?

(iii) What letter is inside the diamond?

(iv) What shape contains the letter U?

(v) What shape contains the letter E?

8 In what way does the grid of numbers below differ from the original?

6	6	6	3	7	7	7	7
6	6	6	3	3	7	1	7
6	9	9	9	3	1	1	7
6	9	2	9	8	1	1	7
4	4	2	9	8	5	5	5
4	4	2	2	8	8	5	8
4	4	2	2	2	8	5	8
4	4	4	4	2	8	8	8

9   Which 3 number plates have you just looked at?

B156CK

F724MS

TI56LN

B724MS

F156LN

T724CK

F389CK

B156MS

10   Which of the following has an identical twin?

11   List six ways in which the following differs from the original.

12   Which of the following have you just looked at?

13   (i)   Which is the only even number in the circle?

(ii) To what number is the black arrow pointing?

(iii) Which number has a white dot underneath it?

(iv) To what number is the white arrow pointing?

(v)   What number has a black dot above it?

14

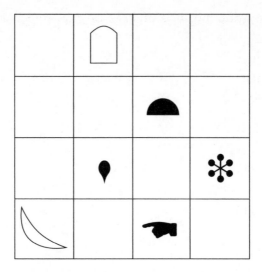

(i)   Which two figures have changed places with each other?

(ii) Which figure has changed from white to black?

(iii) Draw the figure which has disappeared from the original grid.

15

1	Name a tree and a boat	beginning with	C
2	Name a musical instrument and a reptile	beginning with	V
3	Name a vehicle and a dog	beginning with	T
4	Name a plant and a vehicle	beginning with	A
5	Name a boat and a country	beginning with	P
6	Name a tree and a plant	beginning with	H
7	Name a dog and a musical instrument	beginning with	B
8	Name a country and a tree	beginning with	R
9	Name a reptile and a dog	beginning with	S
10	Name a plant and a vehicle	beginning with	M
11	Name a vehicle and a boat	beginning with	F
12	Name a country and a dog	beginning with	L

16   What is the meaning of these boys' names?

1   BRIAN
2   FRED
3   JOHN
4   WALTER
5   THOMAS
6   MARTIN
7   DAVID
8   EDWARD
9   KENNETH
10   PETER

4

Agility of mind

One definition of intelligence is the ability to think quickly, indeed, most intelligence tests set a time limit in which the test must be completed, and if this time limit is not strictly adhered to, then the test score is invalidated. The ability to think quickly and under pressure is a valuable asset to have at one's disposal in many situations.

Agility of mind is the ability to think quickly and react instinctively to certain situations. All the tests in this chapter are speed tests against the clock where in addition to weighing up each situation quickly, you must keep your wits about you, keep calm, and maintain your concentration by dealing with just one question at a time while under pressure.

In psychology, a *speed test* is a general term for any test that measures ability by determining the number of problems that can be dealt with successfully within a fixed time period. According to this definition, therefore, the majority of Intelligence Tests (IQ tests) are speed tests. Opposite to this is a *power test* which is defined as any test that measures ability by determining the degree of difficulty of material that can be mastered with no time pressures on the test taker.

In themselves, the questions contained within the tests that follow are not particularly difficult. However, when presented as a series of questions to be attempted within a set time limit, the brain must adapt to the situation before it and agility of mind plus a great deal of concentration is required in order to score highly.

Questions and tests

Speed test (Answers, see pp. 203–5)

1   The following is a speed test of 30 questions designed to test your powers of mental calculation and logic. In themselves the questions are not particularly difficult but because of the short period of time in which you are allowed to complete the test, alertness and agility of mind are the key ingredients to scoring well, as with all the tests in this section.

It is also necessary in this test to maintain your powers of concentration and keep a clear mind throughout, and maintain your focus on dealing with just one question at a time as quickly as possible.

You have just 60 minutes in which to complete the 30 questions.

(i)   Which two words are anagrams of each other?

salient, leading, reading, aligned, reaping, teasing, trained, realist

(ii)   If the word CAT is written above the word PIG, and the word FOX is written between the words PIG and CAT, what two words are formed diagonally?

(iii)   5632953267846985

Delete all the numbers that appear more than once in the above list and multiply the remaining numbers together. What is the total?

(iv)   What letter in the alphabet comes two before the letter which comes five after the letter that comes three places after the letter H?

(v)   If I walk:

>   3 miles east
>   then 1 mile south
>   then 2 miles east
>   then 1 mile south
>   then 1 mile west
>   then 2 miles north

how far away will I be from my original starting point?

(vi)   If I have £150 and give away 30%, then another £65, how much am I left with?

(vii)   The name of what creature (5 letters long) can be produced from the letters of the word COMPOSITE?

(viii) What is the date 45 days after the 22 March?

(ix)   What is the longest English word that can be produced from the following letters?:

> AMTLOKGB

(x)   A triangle has lengths of 9cm, 12cm and 15cm. What is the value of its largest angle?

(xi)   If a car travels 80 miles in the same time as another car travelling 10mph faster travels 100 miles, what is the speed of the faster car?

(xii)   If Wales has 60%, Birmingham has 70%, Scotland has 75%, Las Vegas has 62.5% and Perth has 80%, what percentage has Dusseldorf?

(xiii) What phrase is suggested by the arrangement of letters below?

    AST
    FKA
    BRE

(xiv)   How many minutes is it before 1p.m. if 20 minutes ago it was three times as many minutes past 11a.m.?

(xv)   What number is 24 less when multiplied by 4 times itself?

xvi)   The names of which two countries can be produced separately by using letters contained within the word TECHNICAL?

(xvii)

27	2	9	24
8	16	6	12
13	35	18	1
10	42	21	4

11	27	9	16
28	19	34	8
21	3	17	13
12	15	6	1

Multiply the third lowest odd number in the right-hand grid by the third highest even number in the left-hand grid.

(xviii) After having spent ⅕ of your original amount and then a further £38 you are left with £58. How much money did you start out with?

(xix)

ADVERB
COAXED
*N*U**
GLITCH

Complete the third word in the list.

(xx)   Which three of the following numbers add up to 100?

36, 42, 35, 26, 29, 34

(xxi)   Arrange these eight words in alphabetical order:

acropolis
adept
accompany
admission
academic
address
adoration
accordion

(xxii)   Which is greater: ⅘ of 190 or ⅜ of 450?

(xxiii)   ACT LITHE is an appropriate anagram of what 8-letter word?

(xxiv)

A   B   D   G   K   ?

What letter comes next?

(xxv)   What number is missing?

1	5	2
4	8	5
2	6	?

(xxvi)   Which is greater, thirteen thousand thirteen hundred and thirteen or fourteen thousand four hundred and four?

(xxvii) Angela's mother has three children, the first is called June, the second is called May. What is the name of her third child?

xxviii) 100, 98, 94, 86, ?

What number comes next?

(xxix) Bill has a fifth as many again as Carol who has a quarter again as many as Ann. Together they have 105. How many has each?

(xxx) Which two numbers in Column A add up to the same amount as two numbers in Column B?

A	B
29	16
14	19
18	29
25	23

Visual sequence test (Answers, see pp. 205–8)

2   The visual sequence puzzles in this test are of varying degrees of difficulty and have been designed to test your creative powers and alertness of mind, in which you must quickly decide what sequences or patterns are occurring.

No options are provided and you must produce a sketch of the missing figures purely based on the evidence presented.

You have 30 minutes in which to complete the 10 questions.

(i)   Draw the next figure in the following sequence.

(ii) Draw the next figure in the following sequence.

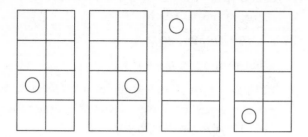

(iii) Draw the next figure in the following sequence.

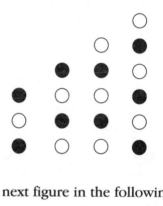

(iv) Draw the next figure in the following sequence.

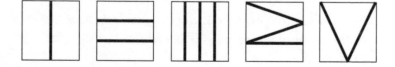

(v) Complete the next two figures in this sequence.

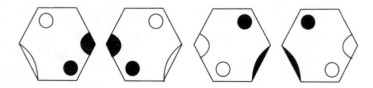

(vi) Complete the blank circles in this pattern.

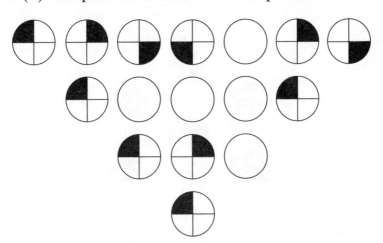

(vii) Complete the next two figures in this sequence.

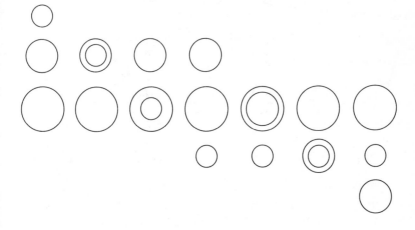

(viii) Draw the next figure in the following sequence.

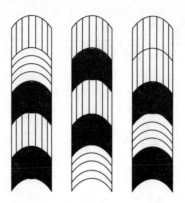

(ix) Draw the next three circles in this sequence.

(x) Draw the next figure in the following sequence.

Mental arithmetic speed test (Answers, see pp. 208–10)

3   It is evident that mental arithmetic is not practised in today's education system to the extent that it was many years ago. Perhaps this is not completely surprising with the widespread use of calculators and computers, nevertheless, the punching of a calculation into a hand-held calculator does not do much to stimulate the brain cells. Several years ago children would learn their multiplication tables so well off by heart that they could

give the answer to sums such as 7 multiplied by 8 or 6 multiplied by 9 almost without thinking, but sadly this is not the case today.

However, we still believe that mental arithmetic is still a valuable asset to have at one's disposal and it is also an excellent way of exercising the brain and keeping your mind alert.

The following is a mental arithmetic speed test of 30 questions which gradually increase in difficulty as the test progresses. Only the answer must be committed to paper, and, of course, the use of calculators is not permitted.

You should work quickly and calmly and try to think at all times of the quickest and most efficient way of solving the questions. As well as agility of mind this is also a test of your ingenuity as there are short cuts to arriving at the correct solution for many of these calculations.

You have 45 minutes in which to solve the 30 questions.

(i)   What is 7 multiplied by 12?

(ii)   What is 144 divided by 3?

(iii)   What is 11 multiplied by 13?

(iv)   What is 70% expressed as a fraction?

(v)   Multiply 8 by 7 and divide by 4.

(vi)   Divide 63 by 9 and add 15.

(vii)   What is 20% of 60 divided by 3?

(viii) What is $\frac{4}{5}$ of 620?

(ix)   What is $\frac{7}{8}$ of 96 plus 17?

(x)   Multiply 7 by 3 by 4.

(xi)   Divide 156 by 13 and add 72 multiplied by 3.

(xii)   Multiply 52 by 21.

(xiii)   What is 9 multiplied by 4 multiplied by 3?

(xiv)   What is 40% of 120 multiplied by 4?

(xv)   Add 15 + 19 + 7 + 3 + 14.

(xvi)   Multiply 3 × 16 and add 43.

(xvii)   What is ⅞ of 56?

(xviii)   Which is the greatest, 70% of 140 or 45% of 200?

(xix)   Multiply 8 × 9 × 3.

(xx)   Add ¾ of 36 to ⅖ of 25.

(xxi)   Multiply 75 by 13.

(xxii)   What is 60% of 550?

(xxiii)   Add 273 to 589.

(xxiv)   Subtract 398 from 957.

(xxv)   Subtract 864 from 1296 and multiply by 2.

(xxvi)   Multiply 56 by 11.

(xxvii)   Subtract ⅘ of 95 from ¾ of 160.

(xxviii) Add 30% of 270 to 4/9 of 81.

(xxix)   Add 7 + 58 + 27 and divide by 4 + 39 + 3.

(xxx)   Divide 756 by 18.

4   In this test we are testing your ability to juggle with
    words and fit them into an interlocking grid. You must
    place all the words in the crossword within 30 minutes
    to satisfactorily complete the task.

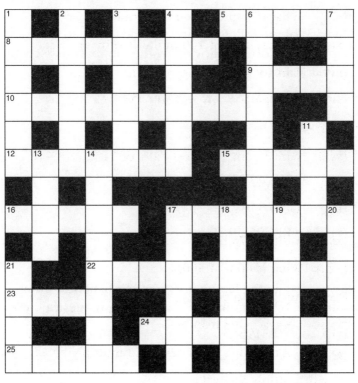

PRODIGY	IDOL	REGIONAL	STATUE
ARENA	ELEVENTH	EMIT	AGOG
APPLAUSE	SLEPT	THEATRE	MENU
ORIGIN	HOLD	CEMENT	ORCHESTRAL
YEARLY	INTONE	TOKEN	TOUGH
RAILROAD	ASPIDISTRA	REPORT	PRIZED
RESCUE	AXLE		

(Answer, see p. 211)

5   This speed test is designed to test your ability to think
     quickly under pressure while keeping a clear mind and at
     the same time absorbing and following instructions. You
     have 20 minutes in which to complete the 20 questions.
     (Answers, see pp. 211–12)

In each of the following arrange the letters in
alphabetical order followed by the numbers in ascending
numerical order:

For example: M35PZ8K = KMPZ358

(i)   2J986PTL

(ii)   49T7SXL3K

(iii)   93BK4TU7W

(iv)   5PE2Z9LG6

(v)   D8KFG964ZL2P

(vi)   MDZ9NT843JB2

Now arrange the letters in reverse alphabetical order,
followed by the numbers in ascending numerical order.

(vii)   8D7JBST95L6

(viii) KF23DJ7PE9W

(ix)   M74PV2S9TKQ

(x)   H2XQJ93UN4G6

Now arrange the letters in reverse alphabetical order,
followed by the numbers in descending order.

(xi)   4CX3YHP79TF

(xii)   2J7KMPB5Q38C4

(xiii) BN2PKFZ3J9RA7

(xiv) 7WG92M3HRV8L5E

Now arrange the letters in forward vowel alphabetical order, then consonants in reverse alphabetical order, followed by numbers in ascending numerical order.

(xv) FTAJU27KE59

(xvi) SE5TU79JZG6B

(xvii) 3J2AFWQUH94ET

Now arrange the consonants in forward alphabetical order, followed by the odd numbers in descending numerical order, followed by the vowels in reverse alphabetical order, followed by the even numbers in ascending numerical order.

(xviii) M35KPA2JUT749D

(xix) 5TW7ADZ3E94RQ6B2

(xx) 6KL9AP732CES5UMJ

Mental verbal dexterity test
(Answers, see pp. 212–13)

6 Look at each set of 7 letters in turn for just 5 seconds, then look away and try to solve the anagram within 2 minutes without committing anything to paper.

This test is designed both to test and develop your powers of memory and your verbal dexterity. To solve each anagram you must first memorise each set of 7 letters and then use these 7 letters to produce a 7-letter English word.

For example: WOKEDRY = KEYWORD

(i) THISROC

(ii) IDLEDYE

(iii)   ITSROLF

(iv)   ITRYJET

(v)   EASYMOD

(vi)   BIDALOT

(vii)   NOGRIEF

(viii) USEDCAR

(ix)   TOREGUM

(x)   BEERCIG

(xi)   DUDHERN

(xii)   ARUDEGP

(xiii) DARNVET

(xiv)   MADMILE

(xv)   MORESKI

(xvi)   ROSECUB

(xvii) ADDRANG

(xviii) IFASUCH

(xix)   THENCAN

(xx)   ISITTEN

(xxi)   RODEGNU

(xxii) ATILLER

(xxiii) IMSONEW

(xxiv) CAFEINN

(xxv)   RAILDOC

Word puzzles test
(Answers, see pp. 214–15)

7   Words are like leaves; and where they most abound,
    much fruit of sense beneath is rarely found.

Alexander Pope

People delight in playing with words – pulling words apart,
reconstructing them in different guises, arranging them in
clever patterns and finding hidden meanings within them.

   It is often said that to have a mastery of words is to have
the ability to produce order out of chaos and that a
command of vocabulary is a true measure of intelligence. As
such, vocabulary tests are widely used in intelligence testing.
In this section we exercise your word power and agility of
mind in restoring order from the chaos we have created in a
variety of 6 different types of word puzzles.

   Each of the puzzles vary in difficulty, and to enable you to
monitor your performance in finding a solution we have
indicated a time limit for each puzzle. If, however, you
cannot solve the puzzle within the set time limit, this is no
cause for despondency. Instead you should persevere and
attempt to solve the puzzle in your own time. The main
purpose of the puzzles in this sub-section is to entertain and
intrigue you, and to give your brain a thorough work-out.

(i)	Cryptic crossword	Time limit: 25 minutes
(ii)	Replace the vowels	Time limit: 10 minutes
(iii)	Trackaround	Time limit: 5 minutes
(iv)	Alphabet crossword	Time limit: 20 minutes
(v)	Enigmagram	Time limit: 8 minutes
(vi)	Anagrams	Time limit: 5 minutes

Cryptic crossword

¹R	E	²E	D	³P	I	⁴P	E	⁵S		⁶C	
E		O		R		R		⁷P	O	O	L
⁸D	⁹A	N	C	E		O		R		L	
	L		¹⁰C	A	B	O	O	D	L	E	
¹¹S	M	O	T	E		E		U		A	
	S			P		¹²S	¹³U	T	U	R	E
¹⁴C	H	E	¹⁵A	T	¹⁶S		K			S	
	O		C		A		¹⁷U	N	I	T	E
¹⁸S	U	I	C	I	D	A	L			U	
	S		E		D		¹⁹E	R	²⁰O	D	²¹E
²²B	E	A	N		L		L		B		G
	S		²³T	E	E	T	E	R	I	N	G

(i)   Find the answers in the crossword above, to solve these 16 cryptic clues.

A   Pay American money into your account, and speak with a dialect

B   Is a lucid thought 'take one's life'.

C   Blunt-edged surgical instruments.

D   Walking the tightrope.

E   Ring the deer to wear away.

F   Musical instruments on the river bank.

G   Hit by tomes.

H   Don't slam the door on these charity abodes.

I   Vegetable that will shoot forth.

J   Lad named Des, places this on his horse.
K   West Indian sorcery found in the Gobi desert.
L   Could be jumping.
M   Urge a hen to produce a spheroid.
N   Give a sachet to the dishonest people.
O   A game played in the water.
P   Get caned and slide around the ballroom.

Replace the vowel

(ii) All of the vowels have been removed from this saying.

Replace them to find the saying.

THMNW   HKNWS   HWWLL   LWYSH   VJBTH
MNWHK   NWSWH   YWLLL   WYSBH   SBSS

Trackaround

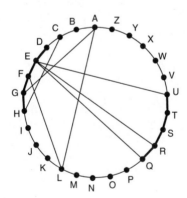

(iii) Clue: They race to it? (9–4)

Trace the letters across the chords and around the
circumference to find two words which form a familiar
phrase.

However, if the next letter is 1–4 letters away from the previous one in the alphabet, then trace around the circumference rather than across the chords.

Alphabet crossword

(iv) Place the 26 letters of the alphabet in the grid to complete the crossword. Seven letters are already in place and one clue is given.

Clue: With all haste (7)

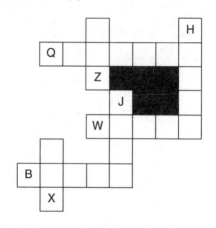

A B̸ C D E F G H̸ I J̸ K L M
N O P Q̸ R S T U V W̸ X̸ Y Z̸

Enigmagram

(v)

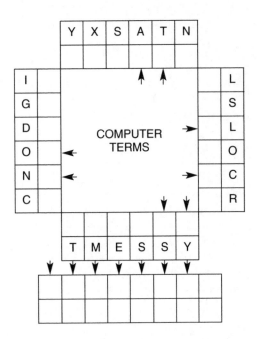

The four six-letter words have been jumbled – solve the four anagrams of computer terms and write the answers in the adjacent spaces. Transfer the arrowed letters to the key anagram and solve the fifth anagram, which is a computer term.

Anagrams

(vi) Each set of 9 squares can be arranged to form a 9-letter word. These are their meanings, not in order.

- RESTAURANT
- DEGREE
- HORSEMAN
- COLD AND GLOOMY

N	E	T	T	E	E
A	U	S	A	C	I
I	N	R	R	F	A
H	A	I	R	E	T
L	C	R	A	O	O
E	E	V	C	D	T

A ... B

C ... D

5

Intelligence tests

An intelligence test (IQ test) is, by definition, any test that purports to measure intelligence. Generally such tests consist of a series of tasks, each of which has been standardized with a large representative population of individuals. Such procedure establishes the average IQ as 100.

IQ tests are part of what is generally referred to as Psychological Testing. Such test content may be addressed to almost any aspect of our intellectual or emotional make-up, including personality, feelings, attitude and intelligence.

It is generally accepted that a person's IQ rating is a hereditary characteristic which barely changes throughout life in adults. In childhood, mental age remains fairly constant in development to about the age of 13, after which it is shown to slow up, and beyond the age of 18 little or no improvement is found.

When measuring the IQ of a child, the subject will attempt an IQ test which has been standardized with an average score recorded for each age group. Thus a child of 10 years of age who scored the results expected of a child of 12 would have an IQ of 120, calculated as follows:

$$\frac{\text{mental age (12)}}{\text{chronological age (10)}} \times \quad 100 \quad = \quad 120 \text{ IQ}$$

However, because in adulthood little or no improvement in IQ rating is found, adults have to be judged on an IQ test whose average score is 100 and their results graded above and below this norm according to known scores.

This chapter consists of two separate IQ tests, each of 40 questions. Within each of these tests are four sub-tests, each of 10 questions, in four different disciplines: spatial ability, logical thought processes, verbal ability and numerical ability. It is these disciplines that are most common in IQ testing.

Because these tests have been specially compiled for this book and have not, therefore, been standardized, an actual IQ rating cannot be given. We do, however, give a performance rating for each test of 10 questions to enable you to identify your own strengths or weaknesses and we also give an overall rating for each complete test of forty questions. It is this overall rating which is the best guide to your IQ rating.

10-question test: (time limit 30 minutes)

Rating:
10   exceptional
8–9   excellent
7   very good
5–6   good
4   average

40-question test (time limit 2 hours)

36–40   exceptional
31–35   excellent
25–30   very good
19–24   good
14–18   average

The first modern intelligence test was devised in 1905 by the French psychologists Alfred Binet and Theodore Simon. The pair developed a 30-item test with the purpose of ensuring that no child be denied admittance to the Paris school system without formal examination.

In 1916 the American psychologist Lewis Terman revised the Binet–Simon scale to provide comparison standards for Americans from age 3 to adulthood. Terman devised the term *intelligence quotient* and developed the so-called Stanford–Binet intelligence test to measure IQ after joining the faculty of Stanford University as Professor of Education. Since revised on a number of occasions, the Stanford–Binet test is today one of the most widely used of all the various intelligence tests in use throughout the world.

While it is generally agreed that IQ is hereditary and remains fairly constant throughout life, it is possible to improve your own performance on IQ tests by regularly practising the different types of tests and questions you are likely to encounter.

An IQ test is set and used on the assumption that those taking the test have little or no knowledge of the testing method itself and that they know very little about the question methods within these tests. It follows, therefore, that if you are able to learn something about this form of testing and know how to approach the different kinds of questions, you can improve your performance on the tests themselves.

In the past 25–30 years IQ tests have been put to widespread use in industry and commerce because of the need by employers to ensure they place the right person in the right job from the outset. One of the main reasons for this is the high cost of errors in today's world of tight budgets and reduced profit margins. To recruit a new member of staff an employer has to advertise, consider each application, reduce the applicants to a short list, interview and then train the successful applicant. If the wrong choice has been made, then the whole expensive and time-consuming process has to be repeated.

Employers also use tests to identify suitable jobs for people within an organization. These tests can be helpful to both the employer and employee in identifying strengths and weaknesses and thus help find the job for which a person is most suited, and can also identify candidates for possible promotion.

Such tests are designed to give an objective assessment of the candidate's abilities in a number of disciplines, for example, in verbal understanding, numeracy, logic and spatial, or diagrammatic, reasoning skills. Unlike personality tests, which are used in conjunction with IQ tests by employers, IQ tests are marked and may have a cut-off point above which you pass, and below which you fail.

Because they are so widely used by employers, improving your IQ rating by a few vital points could mean the difference between success and failure when attending a job interview that includes taking such a test.

Additionally, practice on the type of questions that follow in this section also gives the brain a much needed work-out. Despite the huge capacity of the human brain, we only use, on average, 2 per cent of our potential brainpower. There is, therefore, enormous potential for us to expand our brainpower considerably and regular testing is one of the key methods of doing just that.

IQ test one

Spatial ability test (Answers, see pp. 215–16)

Read the instruction to each question and study each set of diagrams carefully.

 1

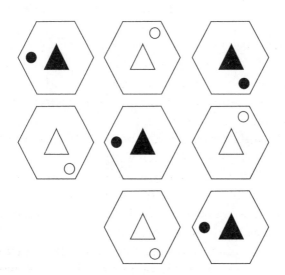

Which is the missing hexagon?

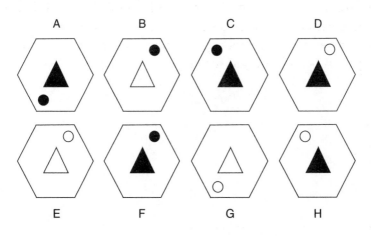

2   Which is the odd one out?

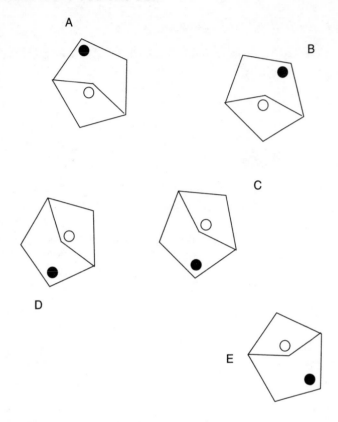

3

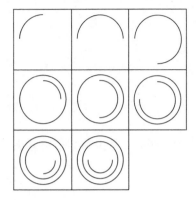

Which is the missing square?

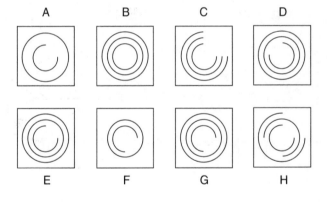

4

Which piece below, when fitted into the piece above, will form a perfect circle?

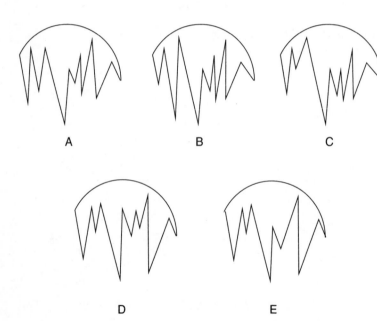

5

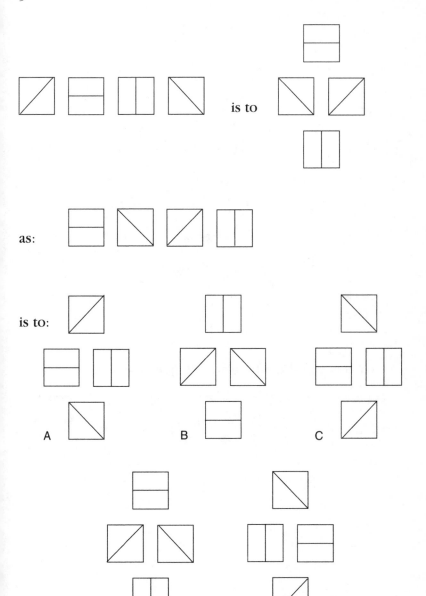

6

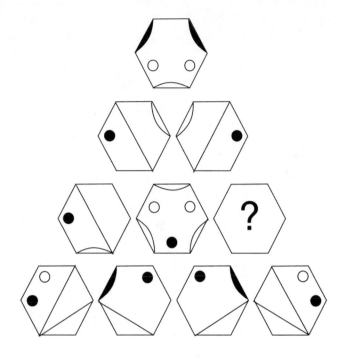

Which hexagon should replace the question mark?

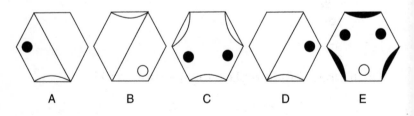

A   B   C   D   E

7

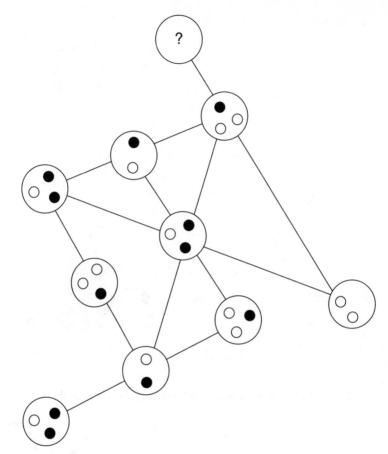

Which circle should replace the question mark?

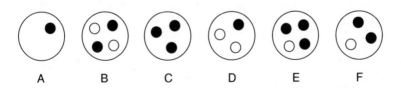

A   B   C   D   E   F

8   Which is the odd one out?

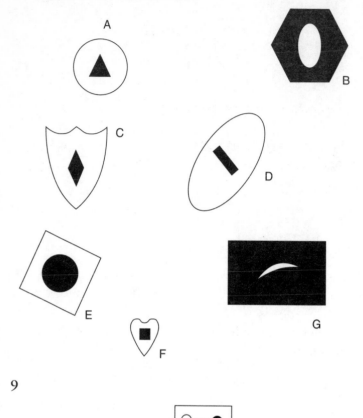

9

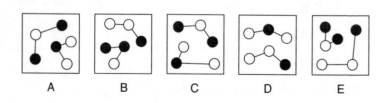

Which box below has most in common with the box above?

10

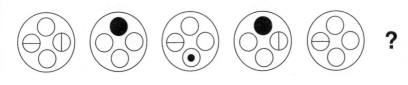

What comes next in the above sequence?

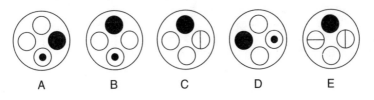

A   B   C   D   E

Logic test (Answers, see pp. 217–19)

1   What is it that occurs once in a blue moon, twice in a lifetime, but never in a month of Sundays?

2   What conclusion can be drawn as a result of the three statements below?

   (i)   No-one has a degree in bio-chemistry unless they went to Oxford.

   (ii) No-one over 30 can speak Spanish and Manx.

   (iii) Those who cannot speak Spanish and Manx did not go to Oxford.

3
        1739482

        8492371

        7321948

   What number continues the sequence?

4   My watch showed the correct time at 12 noon but then
    the battery started to run down until it eventually
    stopped completely.

    Between 12 noon up to it stopping it lost 14 minutes per
    hour on average.

    It now shows 15.50, but it stopped 5 hours ago.

    What is the correct time now?

5   Fill in the missing numbers.

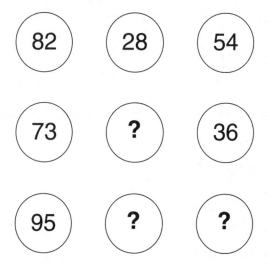

6 Where would you place the letters B, G and L in the grid?

						K		
D								
	E							
				I				
C			H					
				J				
A	F							

7 The following words are in logical progression.

blank

mirage

glisten

portrait

What comes next?

whispered, vacillate, kissogram, reticence, vacate, wisdom

8 In my pocket, all but four of the coins are valued 10 pence, all but four are valued £2, all but four are valued 50 pence, all but four are valued 5 pence and all but four are valued £1.

How much money have I in my pocket?

9   What numbers should replace the question marks?

3	6	8
4	1	9
7	8	7

2	8	3
6	5	8
9	4	1

1	7	4
6	9	8
?	?	?

10   Which four letters do not belong in this group?

ARRK

BAYT

COLL

CORT

HSTY

PIER

SOST

SWOD

THRS

Verbal ability test (Answers, see pp. 219–20)

1   Plight is to predicament as quandary is to:

enigma, imbroglio, dilemma, hitch, conundrum, quagmire

2   Which word in brackets is closest in meaning to the word in capitals?

MUNDANE (cheap, banal, ethereal, dreary, recondite)

3   FILTHY SEASON is an anagram of which two words that
    are synonyms?

4   Complete the circles to find two words that are
    opposite in meaning, one reading clockwise and the
    other anti-clockwise. You must provide the missing
    letters.

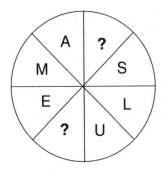 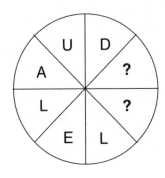

5   Which of these is not an anagram of a country?

    gulp rota

    or yawn

    tact nail

    big Laura

    regain tan

6 Place two letters in each bracket so that they finish the word on the left and start the word on the right. The letters in brackets, when read downwards in pairs, will spell out an 8-letter word.

   SL (**) LE

   TH (**) ED

   MO (**) ON

   PA (**) LL

7 Only one of the following groups of letters can be rearranged to spell a 5-letter English word. Find the word:

   EGIPO

   PTABE

   DILOC

   HUENA

   PLUNO

   OLNEF

   LEMUC

   MTIOW

8 Which two of the following words are most opposite in meaning?

   accurate, erudite, late, ignorant, peripatetic, trivial

9   Working clockwise choose one letter from each circle in turn to spell out two words that are synonyms. Each word starts in a different circle, and every letter is used only once each.

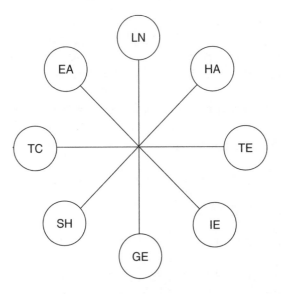

10   Find the starting point and work from letter to adjacent letter horizontally, vertically or diagonally to spell out a 17-letter phrase. Every letter is used only once each.

N	I	R		
G	S	T		
S	A	O	N	H
		T	C	E
		A	T	D

Numerical Ability Test (Answers, see pp. 220–22)

Calculators may be used where preferred

1   What number continues this sequence?

6, 20, 62, 188, **?**

2   How many minutes is it before 12 noon if 5 minutes ago it was 4 times as many minutes past 9a.m.?

3   Harry has a quarter as many again as Dick, and Dick has a third as many again as Tom. Altogether they have 240. How many has each?

4   What number should replace the question mark?

	6	
7	4	
1	9	

	1	
8	3	
2	7	

	6	
?	8	
1	2	

5

14	9	22	7	1
26	6	28	10	3
4	19	2	36	24
16	5	11	8	5
13	18	44	20	12

What number is two places away from itself plus 2, three places away from itself divided by 2, one place away from itself less 2 and three places away from itself multiplied by 2?

6   Insert the numbers 1–6 in the circles, so that for any
    particular circle, the sum of the numbers in the circles
    connected directly to it equals the value corresponding
    to the number in that circle as given in the list.

For example:

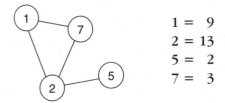

1 = 9
2 = 13
5 = 2
7 = 3

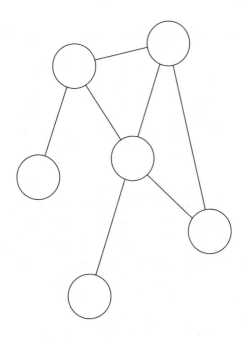

1 = 12
2 = 3
3 = 7
4 = 15
5 = 5
6 = 4

7 What numbers should replace the question marks?

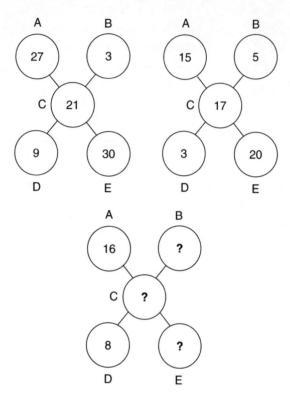

8 A batsman is out for 11 runs, which reduces his batting average per innings for the season from 24 to 23. How many runs would he have needed to score to increase his average from 24 to 27?

9 What numbers should replace the question marks?

A	B	C	D	E
5	4	9	3	5
8	14	9	10	12
22	17	26	20	19
39	48	36	41	46
?	?	?	?	?

10

   1   1   4   9   7   17   10   25   ?   ?

What are the two missing numbers?

IQ test two

Spatial ability test (Answers, see pp. 222–24)

1   What should replace the question mark in hexagon G?

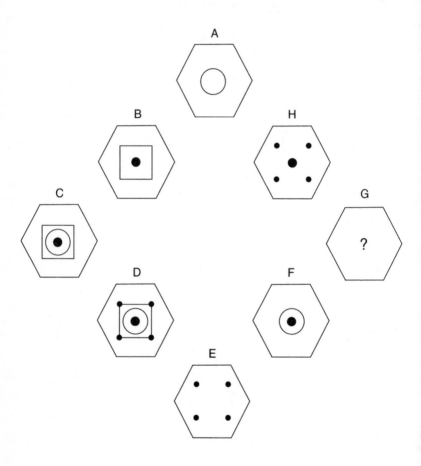

2

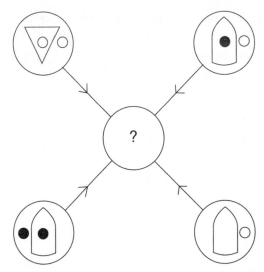

Each line and symbol which appears in the four outer circles, above, is transferred to the centre circle according to these rules:

If a line or symbol occurs in the outer circles:

once:	it is transferred
twice:	it is possibly transferred
3 times:	it is transferred
4 times:	it is not transferred

Which of the circles A, B, C, D, or E shown below should appear at the centre of the diagram, above?

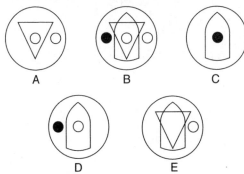

3 Each of the nine squares in the grid marked 1A to 3C, should incorporate all the lines and symbols which are shown in the squares of the same letter and number immediately above and to the left. For example, 3B should incorporate all the lines and symbols that are in 3 and B.

One of the squares is incorrect. Which one is it?

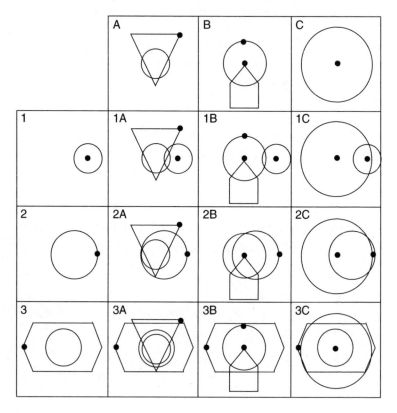

4   Which hexagon should replace the question mark?

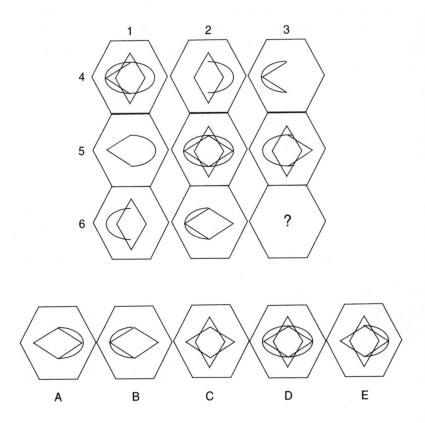

5   Which is the odd one out?

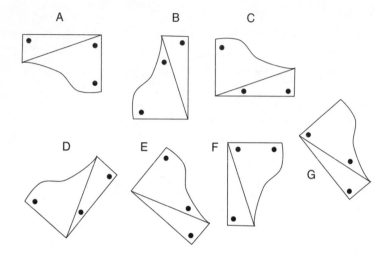

6   Which comes next A, B, C or D?

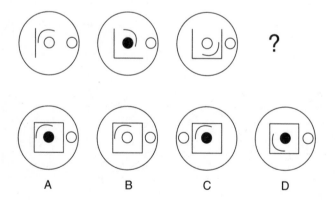

7   Which pentagon should replace the question mark?

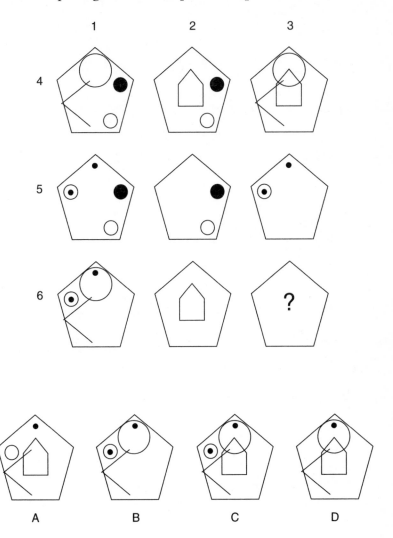

8 Which hexagon should replace the question mark?

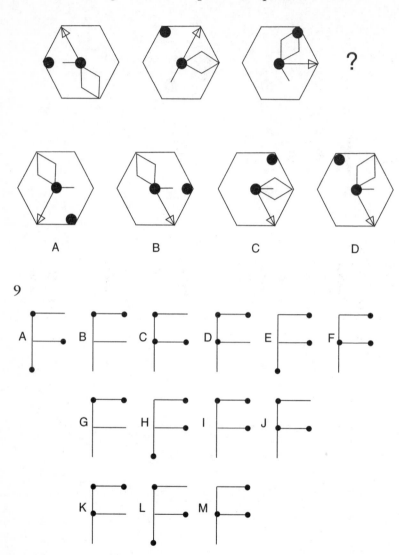

Which is the odd one out?

10

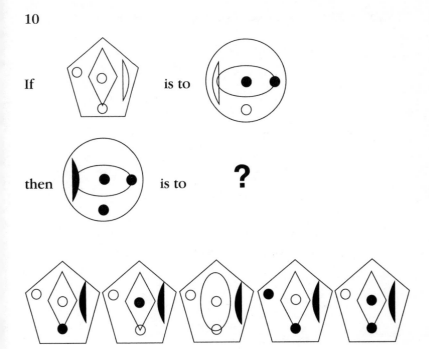

Verbal ability test (Answers, see pp. 224–25)

1   Which is the odd one out?

sepia, magenta, viridian, chamois, maroon

2   REFLECT LANGUAGE is an anagram of which two words
that are similar in meaning?

3   The following clue leads to what pair of rhyming words?

metal refuse container

4   Travel from circle to circle to spell out a 10-letter word.
Use every circle only once each.

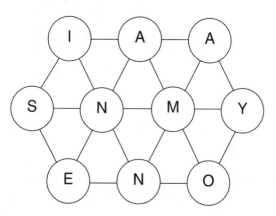

5   Which two words are most opposite in meaning?

uplifted, interpret, refulgence, ostensible,
disfigure, torpid

6 Place the letters in the correct segments in each quadrant
   to obtain two 8-letter related words, one reading
   clockwise, and the other anti-clockwise.

NE : LUTE
SE : TEAR
SW : CORE
NW : TIMP

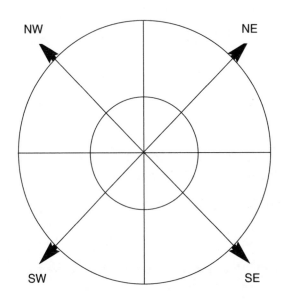

7 Which two words are closest in meaning?

impatient, unmitigated, irrational, matchless,
consummate, coalesce

8

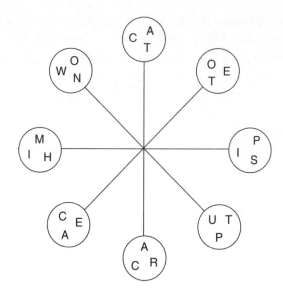

Take one letter from each circle and, reading clockwise, spell out an 8-letter word meaning concise.

You have to find the starting point.

9   TWO SHAKES OF A LAMB'S TAIL

Eliminate 16 letters from the phrase above to leave a word meaning framework.

10   Which two words that sound alike, but are spelled differently mean INTERCEDE, AWARD?

Numerical ability test (Answers, see p. 226)

1   What is the meaning of this mathematical sign?   ∞

      CONGRUENT TO
      INTEGRAL SIGN
      SUMMATION
      INFINITY

2   I have three friends, Clarence, Harold and Peter:

    Clarence's + Harold's age totals 87
    Clarence's + Peter's age totals 75
    Harold's + Peter's age totals 40
    Clarence's + Harold's + Peter's age = 101

    How old are my three friends?

3   A notebook, a pencil, a book and a pen, costs £2.96. The
    notebook costs 55 times the cost of a pencil, and the
    book costs twice the cost of the pen and 160 times the
    cost of a pencil. How much did each cost?

4   Half of twelve is seven as I can show, and half of thirteen
    is eight, can this be so?

5   If 5 times 4 are 33, what will a fourth of 20 be?

6   How many triangles are there in this figure?

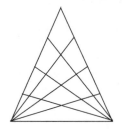

7   7 + 7 + 7 + 7 = 100)

   Using simple mathematical signs make four 7s = 100.

8   The hour and minute hands coincide at noon.

   When will they coincide once again during the next 12 hours?

9   Place the numbers 1, 2, 3, 4, 5, 6, 7, 8, 9, 0 to compose two fractions, whose sum shall be equal to unity. Each number to be used once, and once only.

   <u>Clue</u> $\dfrac{*5}{**} + \dfrac{*4*}{2*6}$

10   What is the difference between six dozen dozen and a half a dozen dozen?

Logic test (Answers, see pp. 227–29)

1   I took my American friend to a cricket match at the Oval in London, 'I do not understand the game,' said the American.

   'Well, Surrey won the championship 5 times out of 9 times in the years running up to the start of the war.'

   'How did they get on in 1930?' said the American.

   'They won in 1931, but did they win or lose in 1930?'

2   Solve this sum:

   $$\frac{16}{22} \div \frac{56}{28} \div \frac{68}{17} \div \frac{26}{13} = x$$

3   If to my age there added be,
    one-half, one-third, and three times three,
    six score and ten the sum you'll see,
    pray find out what my age may be?

4   What number should replace the question mark?

    208, 327, 464, 5125, 6216, ?

5   One shape is missing, what is it?

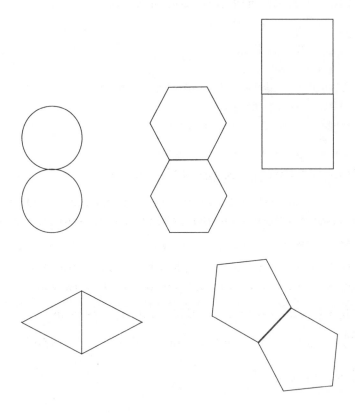

6   What number should replace the question mark?

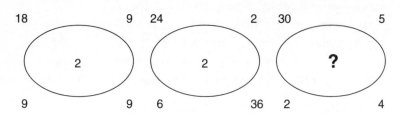

18   9   24   2   30   5

2   2   ?

9   9   6   36   2   4

7   At the car race I did not see the winner of the last race. There were 8 cars in the race, so I asked my friends which number had won.

A said, 'It was odd.'
B said, 'It was even.'
C said, 'It was a prime number.'
D said, 'It was a square number.'
E said, 'It was a cube number.'

1 is not reckoned to be a prime number.

Only one person told the truth.

8   17 coins are tossed in the air.

What are the chances that at least 9 coins will be heads or tails?

9   What weight will a fish weigh if it weighs 37 kg plus half its weight?

10   Divide the square into 4 equal shapes, each shape containing one S, one D, one C and one H.

	S		C		H
	C	H	D		S
	S		D		
		D	S		C
C					D
		H		H	

Hints

Puzzles problem solving

1   If you can figure it out, there is a simple mathematical formula for providing the answer. Start by working out how many different ways the man could travel from West to East if there was just one circular path.

3   Divide the pentagram into the following sections and analyse them.

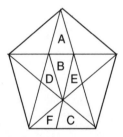

4   Opposite sides of a die always total 7.

5   The full name of one of the guests is Jane Morgan.

6   As in Example 3 at the beginning of this section, write down *all* the possible combinations remaining after a white ball has been drawn out, but remember there are two white balls to consider.

7   Write down the order of floors being visited by the lift. What sequence or sequences emerge?

8   Think of the 3 × 3 array of 9 squares as a magic number square in which each horizontal, vertical and corner-to-corner line add up to the same total.

9   Look at the odd numbers and the even numbers in the sequence separately. Write them down separately. Can you see a sequence occurring?

10   Study each word carefully. Does each reveal part of the message?

11   Look for a relationship between rows of squares.

12   The sum of all the numbers from 1–9 inclusive is 45. The two numbers in the outside circles must, therefore, be 3 and 4.

13   The chance of picking out just one apple which contains a worm is 4 in 50. This would leave just 49 apples in the bag and 3 containing a worm.

14   By joining the dots up in different ways, can a familiar sequence be produced?

15   Looking across and down, what progression is occurring in each row and column?

16   Number the separate segments from 1 to 13.

17   Work out a route back from the black ball to the white ball.

18   I hobbled half as far as I ran.

19   Concentrate on numbers in lines across.

20   Look at the centre of each word.

21   Analyse how many different letters appear in the list of words. If, for example, nine different letters appear, you are looking to form a nine-letter word with these letters, i.e. a nine-letter word that does not repeat a letter.

22   If you are looking for one group of letters that is the odd one out, you must first find what the remaining groups of letters have in common.

23   It is a 1 in 26 chance that the first card will be the letter P.

24   The phrase you are looking for contains 4 × 4-letter words.

25   Look at alternate squares in each row and column.

Numerical problem solving

3   To solve this problem it is necessary to work out how many students studied one language only.

One way of doing this efficiently and quickly is to set up a Venn diagram.

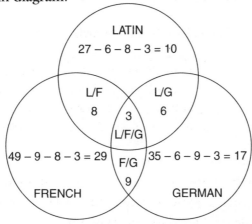

Now see if you can determine the answer from the information you have been given.

4   Work out a hypothetical round of golf with 6 wins to Geoff, 4 wins to Harry and 2 holes tied.

The order of winning makes no difference to the outcome.

5   First, consider the numbers between 200 and 300 that have different factors. For example, 240 fingers could mean:

        20 aliens with 12 fingers
    or 12 aliens with 20 fingers
    or 10 aliens with 24 fingers
    or 24 aliens with 10 fingers

However, this is not a unique answer so it must be eliminated, as must all numbers having different factors.

Carry out a similar analysis with prime numbers. What conclusion do you arrive at?

6   If 3 lied, 3 told the truth.

Analyse my friends' answers with ✓ ticks

Only 3 ✓ will give the correct month.

7   You must calculate the amount of money taken on each horse which will give a margin of 15% on the money staked.

Calculate the amount to be laid on each horse to give a return of £100.

If the total is £115, that means a mark-up of £15 if the bookmaker balances his books.

8   The centre of the coin must fall within a square within the square.

Now try to calculate the odds using this information.

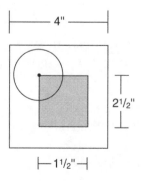

4"

2½"

1½"

9   It would appear that the last number 7, should be an 8
     if the puzzle is:

$$72 + 27 = 99$$
$$27 + 18 = 45$$
$$18 + 21 = 39$$
$$21 + 15 = 36$$
$$15 + 13 = 28$$
$$13 + \ \ 7 = (20?) \ (21?)$$

so the numbers are produced in a different way.

10   To solve this problem you must find the lowest
     common multiple (LCM), that is, the smallest number
     that the number of cog teeth can be divided into.

     The answer is this number divided by the teeth on the
     largest cog.

12 Use Pythagorus' theorem.

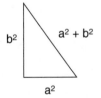

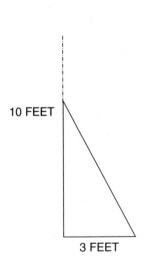

13   Try to find a formula which will provide the answer to this and similar problems.

Calculate the yards travelled for 100-yd maze, 10 squares. Then calculate the yards travelled for an 80-yd maze. This then will give the formula for even squares.

Then calculate a 90-yd square, this will give further parts to the formula.

14   For the puzzle to work, 1,111,111 must have only two factors apart from itself and unity.

Find the factors, they are both prime numbers.

Each factor ends in 9, one factor is under 250.

15   Analyse the numbers 8 to 100, split them up each time into the truth and lies, and find the only unique number that answers the questions.

16   Factorise 6591, and find 7 prime numbers which when multiplied together = 6591.

18   The left-hand side of the equation is divisible by 9 (3^2).

A number is divisible by 9 exactly, only when the sum of its digits is also exactly divisible by 9.

19   The odds of drawing the first correct number is one chance in 49.

The odds of drawing the second correct number is one chance in 48.

Answers

Creativity

Progressive matrices test

1 (i) D: Working round the block of four squares clockwise the figure rotates 90° clockwise and the outside dot alternates white/black.

   (ii) D: Working round the block of four squares clockwise, the black triangle is reducing in size and the white triangle is increasing in size.

   (iii) F: Each square contains three components, inner circle, outer border and middle border. In each row and column these three components are shaded black once each.

   (iv) B: Looking across and down only lines common to both the first two squares are carried forward to the third square.

   (v) D: Looking across and down the contents of the third square are determined by the contents of the previous two squares. Lines which appear in these first two squares are carried forward to the final square, except where lines appear in the same position in these two squares, in which case they are cancelled out.

(vi)   C: So that one of the four different symbols appears in each row and column.

(vii) D: Looking at rows and columns, another circle (or ring), either black or white is added to alternate squares.

(viii) C: Looking along rows, the circle moves from side to side clockwise and, looking down columns, the circle moves to a different side anti-clockwise; in other words, in each row and column the circle is in one of the four different possible positions.

(ix)   D: If you draw a line down the middle of the matrix vertically, the left-hand side is a mirror image of the right-hand side.

(x)   A: So that the left-hand top block of four squares is identical to the right-hand bottom block, and the right-hand top block is identical to the left-hand bottom block.

Rating:
  10 exceptionally creative
   9 very creative
 7–8 well above average
 5–6 above average
 3–4 average

Symbolic interpretation

2   You can mark this test yourself, however, it is best marked by a friend or family member.

Award one mark for each recognizable sketch, providing it is not similar to any of the other sketches. For example, if you draw a face, a second face scores no point as each sketch must have an original theme. You thus obtain marks for variety. If you are creative you will tend to try to draw something different for each sketch.

There is no correct answer to each of the six sketches as for each there is a considerable number of different possible ideas.

Rating

9	exceptionally creative
7–8	very creative
4–6	average

The test can be repeated any number of times either by using the same symbols provided or by using new symbols or lines of your own invention as starting points.

Lateral thinking word puzzles

3   (i)   They contain two consecutive sets of double letters, for example: Carolina **All**spice.

   (ii)   N   I
          T   W

   The letters which appear are the first two letters in the series first, second, third, fourth, fifth, sixth, seventh, eighth, **ni**nth, tenth, eleventh, **tw**elfth.

   (iii)   hand: words in column A can be prefixed with OLD: old faithful, old master, old soldier, old fashioned, old hand. Words in column B can be prefixed with NEW: new broom, new born, new moon.

   (iv)   biography

   The letters ABCDEFGH are contained in the words in the same position as they are in the alphabet, for example, the eighth letter in biography is H, which is the eighth letter of the alphabet.

(v)   rail

Take the initial letters of each word to form words reading both across and down:

DEAR
RARE
ASIA
WEAR

(vi)   They all contain three consecutive letters of the alphabet in reverse order, for example: the Common Market (onm)

(vii) A

Read down from top to right to spell out the words: arcane, crane, near, ran, an, a.

(viii) They all form words when a letter is deleted from the end one at a time, for example, herons, heron, hero, her, he and notes, note, not, no.

(ix)   elope ruler (Peru)
formal tacit (Malta)
governor wayfarer (Norway)

(x)   Insert numbers into each group of letters to form a word:

LISS + ONE = LIONESS
NERK + TWO = NETWORK
WED + EIGHT = WEIGHTED
ZASS + NINE = ZANINESS
EXD + TEN = EXTEND

The circles of your mind

4   If you study the design carefully you will see that regular patterns of circles appear in the three circular rings in order to give the whole design symmetry. For example, in the middle ring, every fourth circle contains a dot, every fourth circle contains a stripe and every sixth circle is black. The remaining circles are white, which lie directly opposite each other.

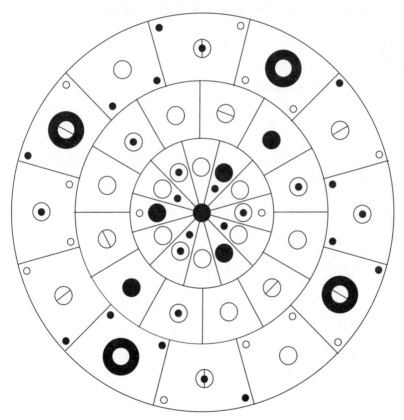

Divergent ability

5   Scoring and analysis:

You can mark your efforts yourself, but it is better if you get a friend or family member to do so.

Allow:
2 points for any good or original answer
1 point for a good attempt
0 points for completely impractical answers

Rating:
18–24   highly creative
13–17   above average
 7–12   average

Now repeat the exercise as many times as you wish using other everyday objects, for example, a paper clip or an A4 piece of cardboard.

Rebuses

6   (i)   Despair

(ii)   Colonel (colon L)

(iii)   Short measure

(iv)   Square meal

(v)   One word
   1 backwater
   2 brainwave
   3 groundhog (G round hog)
   4 laundrette (la under ette)
   5 backgammon
   6 printout (pr in tout)

(vi) Familiar phrases
1 world without end
2 simple fracture
3 central nervous system
4 winds of change
5 next to nothing
6. tree of knowledge
7 quarter sessions
8 to go over board
9 mixed doubles (lobsdue is an anagram of doubles)
10 through thick and thin
11 fall flat
12 chief constable (chief cons table)

The hidden star

7

Lateral thinking number puzzles

8   (i)   6

The three numbers appearing in the same
position in the three squares all add up to 10.

(ii)   11

Each number represents the numbers in the same
line across and the same line down, for example,
11 means one other number in the same line across
and one other number in the same line down.

(iii)   2836
1063
136
46
10
1

Add the first two numbers and then reverse the rest.

(iv)   0

Take the difference between the sum of numbers
circled and numbers not circled in overlapping
circles. This produces the number in each
overlapping segment.

(v)   5   4

In each line, the numbers in inverted and upright
triangles total 16.

(vi)   1

$7 + 4 = 11$
$12 + 9 = 21$
$15 + 18 = 33$
$15 + 7 = 22$

(vii) 14

The numbers in the bottom half are the sum of the digits of the numbers in the top half as shown below:

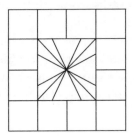

(viii) 28

82

Start at the top and work from left to right, then back along the second row right to left, etc, repeating the digits 58236.

(ix)

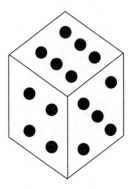

The diagram shows a die being rolled from side to side through four turns from top to bottom.

(x)   1813

> Looking top left to bottom right, add even numbers only to obtain the first part of the middle number. Looking top right to bottom left, add odd numbers only to obtain the second part of the middle number. That is: $6 + 8 + 4 = 18$ and $5 + 1 + 7 = 13$.

Situation puzzles

10   Explanations:

(i)   He is an official delivering a last-minute pardon to a prisoner on death row. The flicker of the lights indicated that the prisoner has just been electrocuted and the pardon has arrived too late.

(ii)   The man is a postman delivering mail to the capitol's foreign embassies.

(iii) The two men started at opposite sides of the trench digging towards each other, but instead of meeting in the middle they dig right past each other because one of them has failed to dig in a straight line. Their boss confirms that one man was right after inspecting the plans and orders that the other man must re-dig his half of the trench.

(iv)   Doris was a pet mouse sitting on a chair. Alan was playing musical chairs and sat down quickly when the music stopped, not noticing that Doris had climbed on to the chair.

(v)   Harry is a child. Last year he could only reach the 11th floor button. This year he can reach the 12th floor button.

(vi) They are in a drive-in movie, so the crime goes undetected.

(vii) The man was a night-watchman who should have been on duty last night, and not dreaming.

(viii) It is a baker's shop in France. The French word for *bread* is *pain*.

(ix) I am driving my car in reverse.

(x)   He is sitting on the window ledge inside his room.

Sequential patterns

11   (i)

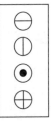

The second circle moves to the bottom at the next stage.

(ii)

Looking across and down, any lines common to the first two squares are not carried forward to the end square, but all other lines are carried forward.

(iii)

Each row and column contains a black centre, a black middle ring, a black outer ring, a black dot below the main circle and a white dot at the top.

(iv)

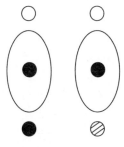

Looking across, the top dot alternates white/black, the dot in the ellipse alternates black/cross and the dot below alternates white/striped/black.

(v)

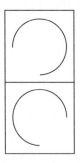

Looking across, the arc rotates 90° clockwise and looking down it rotates 90° anti-clockwise.

(vi)

The figure is rotating 90° clockwise and every alternate figure has a black dot.

(vii)

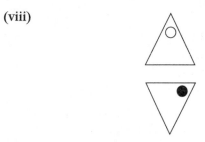

Looking across and down only dots common to the first two squares are carried forward to the third square.

(viii)

The top dots are moving a corner at a time clockwise and the bottom dots anti-clockwise. Both dots alternate black/white.

(ix)

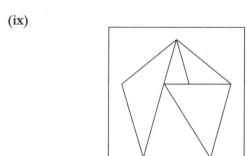

Adjacent figures are
mirror images of
each other.

(x)

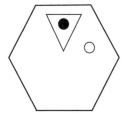

The triangle moves two sides anti-clockwise, the white dot
moves one side clockwise and the black dot moves one side
anti-clockwise.

Rating:
10	exceptionally creative
9	very creative
7–8	well above average
5–6	above average
3–4	average

Matchstick puzzles

12   (i)

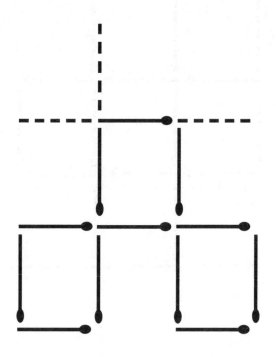

(ii)

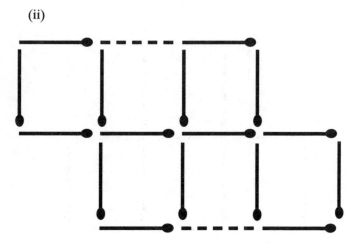

(iii)

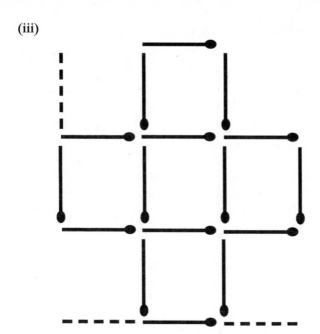

(iv)

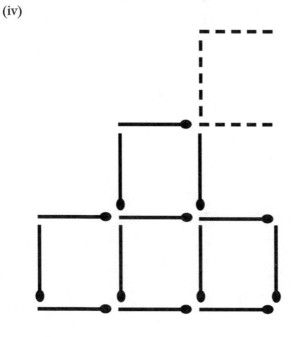

(v)

(vi)

Problem solving

Puzzles

1   $6^3 = 216$

Explanation:

If there was only one circular path the man could continue
in three ways when first reaching the intersection (left, right
or straight forward). On reaching the second intersection he
would have the choice of just two routes, so that altogether
there would be six (3 × 2) possible routes. If the number of
circular routes were increased to two, the choice of routes is
6^2, or 36. With three circular routes the choice of routes is
6^3, or 216. This formula holds good for any number of
circular routes.

2

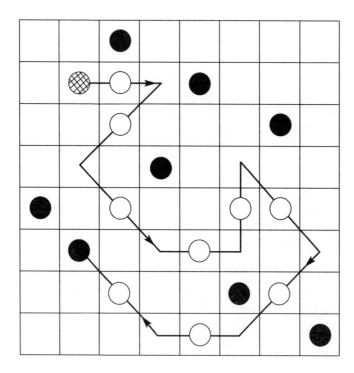

3   Twice the area.

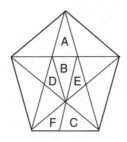

Explanation:

A = B = C and D = E = F

Therefore: A + B + D + E must be twice the area of C + F.

4   27

Explanation:

Because opposite sides of a die always total 7, the bottom face of the top die must be 6 (7+1). Faces 2 + 3, 4 + 5 and 6 + 7 must all total 7. The total of the 7 faces is, therefore, 7 + 7 + 7 + 6 = 27.

5   Four people

Explanation:

My wife and I
Keith, my son
Jane, my sister-in-law

Jane's brother-in-law and his wife are my wife and I.
My book editor Alex is my wife.
Mrs Morgan is my sister-in-law Jane.
Jane's nephew is my son Keith.

6 Two chances in three.

Explanation:

Call the balls which may be put in the bag first W1 and B, and call the white ball that you see go in W2. After the white ball has been drawn out there are three possibilities remaining:

(a)   W1 still in the bag W2 outside.
(b)   W2 still in the bag W1 outside.
(c)   B still in the bag W2 outside.

There are, therefore, only two of the three possibilities where the ball remaining in the bag is white, and one possibility where it is black.

7 14th floor.

Explanation:

It was operating in the sequence 7, 9, 6, 11, 4, 12, 3, 14.

There were, therefore, two alternate sequences, up and down. The down sequence progressed -1, -2, -1, etc.; and the up sequence progressed +2, +1, +2, etc. It would take us to the 14th floor whether we liked it or not.

8 D

Explanation:

Count the number of lines in each square. The number of lines in each horizontal, vertical and corner-to-corner line adds up to 15.

9 29347

Explanation:

Even numbers 6824 and odd numbers 93715 are being repeated in the same order.

10   See me at two by the cliff.

Explanation:

be(see)ch, la(me)nt, C(at)hy, foo(two)rn, a(by)ss, wi(the)er, Heath(cliff)e

11   C

Explanation:

The top row is a mirror image of the third row, and the second row is a mirror image of the bottom row.

12

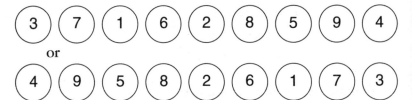

or

13   1 chance in 4900

Explanation:

$$\frac{4}{50} \times \frac{3}{49} \times \frac{2}{48} = \frac{24}{117600} = \frac{1}{4900}$$

14

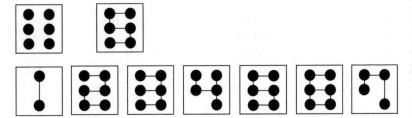

The dots can be joined to produce the sequence of numbers 1 2 3 4 5 6 7.

15   B

Explanation:

Looking across and down in each row and column the number of sides in each figure increases by 1 each time.

16   32

Explanation:

Triangles are formed as follows:

individual triangles	two segments	three segs.	four segs.
1	1/2	1/2/3	2/6/7/10
2	1/4	1/4/5	4/7/8/12
3	2/3	3/8/9	
4	3/8	5/6/11	
5	4/5	9/10/13	
6	5/6	11/12/13	
8	8/9		
9	9/10		
10	6/11		
11	10/13		
12	11/12		
13	12/13		

17

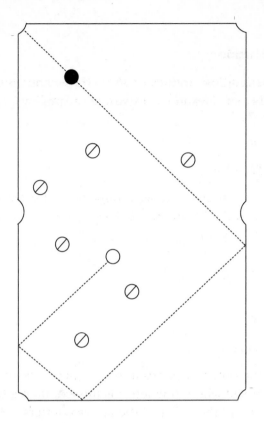

18 Four times faster

Explanation:

I hobbled the last third of the way i.e. half as far as I ran, in twice the time.

For example, suppose the race was 12 miles long.

Then I ran 8 miles and hobbled 4 miles.

Say I ran at 8 mph and walked at 2 mph.

Then: 8 miles at 8 mph = 1 hour
             4 miles at 2 mph = 2 hours

19   7

Explanation:

The middle two lines total 13, the second and fourth lines total 10 and the top and bottom lines total 7.

20   Mexico

Explanation:

Take the Roman numeral value from the centre of each word and add; so that review + envoi = Mexico (vi + v = xi).

21   handsomely

22   JLNM

Explanation:

All the others proceed in the sequence as, for example, LmNoQP where one letter is missed, then a further letter and the order of the last two letters is reversed.

23   358799 to 1

Explanation:

It is a 1 in 26 chance that the first card will be P, 1 in 25 that the second will be A, 1 in 24 the third will be U and 1 in 23 the fourth will be L.

The chances are $26 \times 25 \times 24 \times 23 = 1$ in 258800, or 358799 to 1.

The chances that the last four cards will spell P_A_U_L is exactly the same.

24   Make both ends meet.

Explanation:

Take the first letters of the words in the top row, the second letter of the words in the second row, the third letter of the words in the third row and the fourth letter of the words on the fourth row to spell out the message.

25

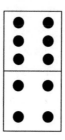

Explanation:

In each row and column alternate pips add up to the same, for example, in the first row, 1 + 6 = 5 + 2.

Numerical problem solving

1   4

Explanation:

If half of 5	=	3
Then $2\frac{1}{2}$	=	3
Then 10	=	12
Then $\frac{1}{3} \times 12$ =		4

2   No

Explanation:

$0 + 1 + 2 + 3 + 4 + 5 + 6 + 7 + 8 + 9 = 45$

Since Jimmy has only 44 the answer is No.

3   18

Explanation:

Latin	10
French	29
German	17
Latin/French	8 L/F
French/German	9 F/G
Latin/German	6 L/G
Latin/French/German	3 L/F/G
	82

100 less than 82 means that 18 students studied none of
the three languages.

4

Hole		Geoff	Harry	
		£100		£0
1	WIN	£150	LOSE	−£50
2	WIN	£225	LOSE	−£125
3	LOSE	£112	WIN	−£13
4	TIE	£112	TIE	−£13
5	LOSE	£56	WIN	+£43
6	WIN	£84	LOSE	+£15
7	WIN	£126	LOSE	−£27
8	LOSE	£63	WIN	+£36
9	LOSE	£32	WIN	+£68
10	WIN	£48	LOSE	+£52
11	WIN	£72	LOSE	+£28
12	TIE	£72	TIE	+£28
	LOSES	£28	WINS	£28

The reason is that if Geoff won every hole he would win thousands of pounds but Harry could only win the £100 in Geoff's wallet. So Harry would win even if he lost by a few holes, to balance the books.

5   As suggested in the hint, if you needed to use it, first, consider numbers between 200 and 300 that have different factors. For example, 240 fingers that could be:

      20 aliens with 12 fingers
   or 12 aliens with 20 fingers
   or 10 aliens with 24 fingers
   or 24 aliens with 10 fingers

Not a unique answer, so all numbers having different factors are eliminated.

Now try prime numbers (a prime number is a number which has no factors except 1 and itself). For example, 233. That could be:

> 1 alien with 233 fingers (but there is more than 1 alien)
>
> or 233 aliens with 1 finger (but each alien has at least 2 fingers)

Not a unique answer, so all prime numbers in the range are eliminated. That leaves only the square of a prime number.

There is only one between 200 and 300 and that is 289 = 17 × 17, so the answer is 17 aliens each with 17 fingers.

6 July

	Alan	Barbara	Carol	David	Edward	Fiona
JAN	✓			✓	✓	✓
FEB					✓	✓
MAR		✓		✓		
APR		✓	✓			
MAY				✓		✓
JUN	✓		✓			
JUL	✓			✓		✓
AUG				✓		
SEP			✓		✓	
OCT				✓	✓	
NOV			✓		✓	
DEC				✓	✓	

As it is the only month with three ticks, the circus must be coming to town in July.

7   Answer: 5–1

   Explanation:

HORSE	ODDS	STAKE(£)
SANDS OF TIME	2–1	33.3
LITTLE BEN	3–1	25.0
MOONSHINE	4–1	20.0
PHIL'S FOLLY	8–1	11.1
ABANDON ALL HOPE	10–1	9.1
CATCH KEN	5–1	16.7
		115.2

   Therefore, as he pays out £100, he collects £115 and
   gives himself a 15% margin.

8   For a coin to fall within a square, its centre must fall
   within the shaded area. If it falls outside, it will touch a
   line. Therefore:

	successful	$1\frac{1}{2} \times 1\frac{1}{2} =$	$2\frac{1}{4}$
	unsuccessful	$16 - 2\frac{1}{4}$	$= 13\frac{3}{4}$
	odds	$13\frac{3}{4} : 2\frac{1}{4}$	
or	odds of	55:9 against	

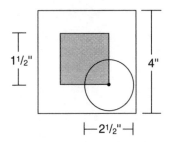

9 12

Explanation:

The numbers are obtained by adding the *digits*, not the *numbers*, so the missing number is 12:

7 + 2 + 9 + 9 = 27
2 + 7 + 4 + 5 = 18
1 + 8 + 3 + 9 = 21
2 + 1 + 3 + 6 = 12

10 56

13	1 × 13
8	2 × 2 × 2
7	~~1~~ × 7
4	~~2 × 2~~

Cross out the repeats, which completely eliminates the smallest cog from the equation.

$$13 \times 8 \times 7 = \frac{728}{13} = 56$$

11   64 diamonds and 8 sons

```
            64
        –    1
            63
    ÷ 9     7
            56
        –    2
            54
    ÷ 9     6
            48
        –    3
            45
    ÷ 9     5
            40
        –    4
            36
    ÷ 9     4
            32
        –    5
            27
    ÷ 9     3
            24
        –    6
            18
    ÷ 9     2
            16
        –    7
             9
    ÷ 9     1
             8
        –    8
             0
```

12 $4^{11}/_{20}$ ft

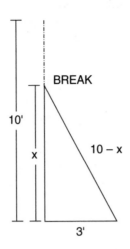

Explanation:

If the height of the break is x:
then
$$x^2 + 3^2 = (10 - x)^2$$

$$10 - x$$

$$\underline{10 - x}$$

$$100 - 10x + x^2$$

$$\underline{- 10x}$$

$$100 - 20x + x^2 = x^2 + 3^2$$

$$- 20x \qquad = -100 + 9$$

$$20x \qquad = 100 - 9$$

$$x \qquad = 5 - \frac{9}{20}$$

$$x \qquad = 4 \frac{11}{20} \text{ ft}$$

13

10 units

10
units

Explanation:

1	9½	14	3
2	9	15	3
3	9	16	2
4	8	17	2
5	8	18	1
6	7	19	1½
7	7		
8	6		
9	6	100 units = 10 units²	
10	5		
11	5	Formula length of walk = side²	
12	4		
13	4	Answer = 60 ft = 3600 ft	

14   1,111,111 = 239 × 4649

Therefore, 239 cats each caught 4649 mice.

15   81

Explanation:

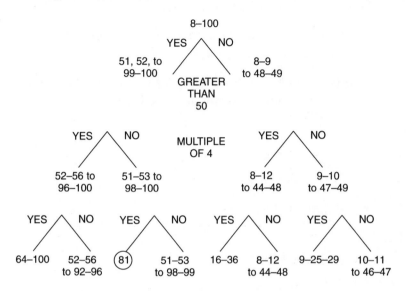

Thus, 81 is the only unique number.

16   $1 \times 1 \times 1 \times 3 \times 13 \times 13 \times 13 = 6591$

Including 2 sets of triplets.

17   To divide by 2.236 is tedious. Avoid this as follows:

$$\frac{3}{\sqrt{5}} \times \frac{\sqrt{5}}{\sqrt{5}} = \frac{3 \times \sqrt{5}}{5}$$

$$= \frac{3 \times 2.236}{5}$$

$$= \frac{6.708}{5}$$

$$= 1.342$$

18   8

>   The left-hand side of the equation is divisible by 9 (3^2), so the right-hand side must also be so.

>   The sum of the digits on the right-hand side is therefore divisible by 9, making ? = 8.

>   Note: a number is divisible by 9 exactly only when the sum of its digits is exactly divisible by 9.

19    $\dfrac{49 \times 48 \times 47 \times 46 \times 45 \times 44}{1 \times 2 \times 3 \times 4 \times 5 \times 6}$

= $\dfrac{1006834752}{720}$

=   13,983,815 to 1

20   19.2 sq yds

Let x = total area

Then $\dfrac{x}{3} + \dfrac{x}{4} + 8 = x$

x12 = 7x + 96 = 12x

$\qquad$ 5x = 96

$\qquad\qquad$ x = $19\frac{1}{5}$ sq yds

Agility of mind

1 (i)   leading/aligned

(ii)   COG and TOP

(iii)   28 (7 × 4)

(iv)   N

(v)   4 miles

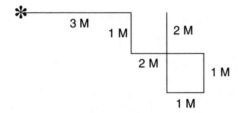

(vi)   £40

(vii)   moose

(viii)   6 May.

(ix)   gambol

(x)   90°

It is a right-angled triangle: 8^2(81) + 12^2 (144) = 15^2 (225)

(xi)   50mph (length of journey = 2 hours)

(xii)   70% (percentage of consonants)

(xiii)   a square meal (breakfast)

(xiv)   25 minutes

       1 p.m. less 25 minutes = 12.35
       12.35 less 20 minutes = 12.15
       12.15 less 75 minutes (3 x 25) = 11 a.m.

(xv)   8

(xvi)   China and Chile

(xvii)   162 (9 × 18)

(xviii)   £120

(xix)   engulf

The words begin and end with consecutive letters of the alphabet ABCDEFGH.

(xx)   36   29   35

(xxi)   academic, accompany, accordion, acropolis, address, adept, admission, adoration

(xxii)   ⅘ of 190 = 152

       ⅓ of 450 = 150

(xxiii)   athletic

(xxiv)   P

       ABcDefGhijKlmnoP

(xxv)   3

       Looking across the sequence is +4, −3.
       Looking down the sequence is +3, −2.

(xxvi)

13000	14000
1300	400
13	4
14313	14404

(xxvii)   Angela

(xxviii) 70

Deduct 2, then 4, then 8, then 16.

(xxix)   Ann 28, Carol 35, Bill 42

(xxx)   14 + 25 = 16 + 23

Rating:
27–30	superb effort
24–26	excellent
20–23	very good
16–19	good
12–15	above average
9–11	average

2   (i)

The diamond moves round a notch at a time as does the black segment.

(ii)

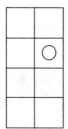

The white dot moves four segments round the rectangle anti-clockwise at each stage.

(iii)

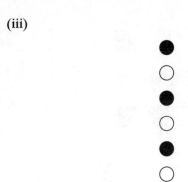

Add a white dot to the bottom, then a white dot to the top, then a black to the bottom and finally a black to the top.

(iv)

The Roman numerals I, II, III, IV, V, VI appear turning 90° clockwise at each stage.

(v)

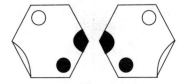

The figures alternate mirror image then black/white reversal.

(vi)

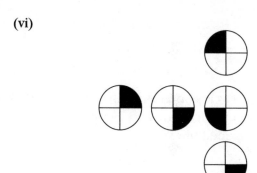

In each row the black segment is moving one segment clockwise.

(vii)

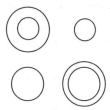

The circles are moving from top to bottom in turn.

 viii)

At each stage the figure next to top drops to the bottom.

(ix)

Every alternate circle contains a white dot, every third circle contains a vertical line and every fourth circle contains a horizontal line.

(x)

The first figure 8 appears a quarter at a time, and a second figure 8 appears a quarter at a time as soon as the first figure 8 starts to disappear.

Rating:
  10 very impressive
   9 exceptional
 7–8 excellent
   6 very good
   5 good
   4 average

3   Some suggested short cuts are indicated for several of the calculations.

  (i)   84

  (ii)   48

  (iii)   143 (10 × 13 = 130 + 13 = 143)

  (iv) $7/10$

(v)   14 (divide 8 by 4 and multiply by 7).

(vi)   22

(vii)   4 (10% of 60 is 6, therefore 20% is 12 and 12 divided by 3 is 4).

(viii)   496

(ix)   101

(x)   84

(xi)   228 (15 divided by 13 is 1 and 2 carried. 26 divided by 13 = 2, therefore 156 divided by 13 = 12. 70 × 3 = 210 plus 2 × 3 = 6, therefore 72 × 3 = 216. 216 + 12 = 228).

(xii)   1092 (52 × 10 = 520 × 2 = 1040. Therefore 20 × 52 = 1040 plus the other 52 = 1092).

(xiii)   108

(xiv)   192

(xv)   58

(xvi)   91

(xvii)   49

(xviii) 70% of 140 = 98, 45% of 200 = 90

(xix)   216

(xx)   37

(xxi)   975 (2 × 75 = 150, therefore 4 × 75 = 300, therefore 12 × 75 = 900, then add the remaining 75 = 975).

(xxii) 330 (10% of 550 = 55. 55 × 6 = 330).

(xxiii) 862 (273 + 600 = 873 less 11 = 862).

(xxiv) 559

(xxv) 864

(xxvi) 616 (56 × 10 = 560 plus the remaining
56 = 616).

(xxvii) 44

(xxviii) 117

(xxix) 2

(xxx) 42

Rating:
28–30 excellent
25–27 very good
22–24 good
19–21 above average
14–18 average

4

R		R		C		S		A	R	E	N	A
E	L	E	V	E	N	T	H		A			X
P		S		M		A		I	D	O	L	
O	R	C	H	E	S	T	R	A	L			E
R		U		N		U		R		A		
T	H	E	A	T	R	E		T	O	U	G	H
	O		P					A		O		
S	L	E	P	T		P	R	O	D	I	G	Y
	D		L			R		R		N		E
E			A	S	P	I	D	I	S	T	R	A
M	E	N	U		Z		G		O			R
I		S			R	E	G	I	O	N	A	L
T	O	K	E	N		D		N		E		Y

5

(i) JLPT2689

(ii) KLST3479

(iii) BKTUW3479

(iv) EGLPZ2569

(v) DFGKLPZ24689

(vi) BDJMNTZ23489

(vii) TSLJDB56789

(viii) WPKJFED2379

(ix)   VTSQPMK2479

(x)   XUQNJHG23469

(xi)   YXTPHFC9743

(xii)   QPMKJCB875432

(xiii)   ZRPNKJFBA9732

(xiv)   WVRMLHGE987532

(xv)   AEUTKJF2579

(xvi)   EUZTSJGB5679

(xvii)   AEUWTQJHF2349

(xviii) DJKMPT9753UA24

(xix)   BDQRTWZ9753EA246

(xx)   CJKLMPS9753UEA26

6   (i)   ostrich

    (ii)   yielded

    (iii)   florist

    (iv)   jittery

    (v)   someday

    (vi)   tabloid

    (vii)   foreign

    (viii)   crusade

    (ix)   gourmet

    (x)   iceberg

(xi)   hundred

(xii)   upgrade

(xiii)   verdant

(xiv)   dilemma

(xv)   irksome

(xvi)   obscure

(xvii)   grandad

(xviii)   fuchsia

(xix)   enchant

(xx)   tiniest

(xxi)   undergo

(xxii)   literal

(xxiii)   winsome

(xxiv)   finance

(xxv)   cordial

Cryptic crossword

7	(i)	A	ACCENT (A/C CENT)	15D
		B	SUICIDAL (ANAGRAM) IS A LUCID	18A
		C	PROBES	4D
		D	TEETERING	23A
		E	ERODE (ANAGRAM) DEER + O	19A
		F	REED PIPES (REED – RIVER BANK)	1A
		G	SMOTE (ANAGRAM) TOMES	11A
		H	ALMS HOUSES (ANAGRAM) SLAM	9D
		I	SPROUT	5D
		J	SADDLE (ANAGRAM) DES + LAD	16D
		K	OBI (G – OBI)	20D
		L	BEAN	22A
		M	EGG	21D
		N	CHEATS (ANAGRAM) SACHET	14A
		O	POOL	7A
		P	DANCE (ANAGRAM) CANED	8A

Replace the vowels

(ii)   THE MAN WHO KNOWS HOW WILL ALWAYS HAVE A JOB.
THE MAN WHO KNOWS WHY WILL ALWAYS BE HIS BOSS.

Trackaround

(iii) Chequered flag

7   (iv)

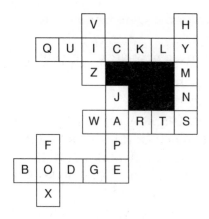

Enigmagram

(v) SYNTAX
SCROLL
SYSTEM
CODING

KEY ANAGRAM = TERMINAL

Anagrams

(vi) A   SATURNINE
B   CAFETERIA
C   CHEVALIER
D   DOCTORATE

IQ test one

Spatial ability test

1   F: In each row and column the triangle alternates
black/white. In each row the dot moves two corners
clockwise and alternates black/white. In each column
the dot moves two corners anti-clockwise and alternates
black/white.

2   B: the rest are the same figure rotated.

3   E: in each row a new circle is building up a quarter at a
    time.

4   D

5   E: the four blocks are rearranged as in the example, i.e.
    left to middle right, second to top, third to bottom,
    right to middle left.

6   D: split the pyramid into two halves vertically. The left-
    hand side is a mirror image of the right-hand side.

7   C: so that each connected line of three circles contains
    four white and four black dots.

8   E: in all the others the part with curved lines is white
    and the part with straight lines is black.

9   E: it contains a string which is black/white/black, and a
    string which is white/white/black.

10 B: looking across, the top circle within the large circle
    alternates white/black, the left-hand circle alternates
    horizontal stripe/white, the right-hand circle alternates
    horizontal stripe/white/white, the bottom circle
    alternates white/white/dot.

Logic test

1   The letter E.

2   No-one over 30 has a degree in bio-chemistry.

3   4918237

Reverse the 4th, 5th and 6th digits from the previous number followed by the 1st, 2nd, 3rd and 7th digits in reverse.

4   It stopped at 15.50.

Explanation:

12 noon	=	12 noon
1 p.m.	=	12.46
2 p.m.	=	13.32
3 p.m.	=	14.18
4 p.m.	=	15.04
5 p.m.	=	15.50 stopped
plus 5 hours	=	10 p.m.

5   82   28   54
    73   37   36
    95   59   36

In each line reverse the numbers then take the difference, i.e. 95 − 59 = 36.

6

Start at A then work up the first column then down the second, etc., first omitting no space, then 1 space, then 2, etc. before adding successive letters of the alphabet.

7   vacillate

Increase each word by one letter. First letter is two after the last letter of previous word in the alphabet.

8   £3.65:

```
 .10
2.00
 .50
 .05
1.00
3.65
```

9   872

174 + 698 = 873. Similarly, 283 + 658 = 941 and 368 + 419 = 787.

10   ARRK

Explanation:

When TWO is inserted into ARRK, the word AR*TWO*RK is produced.

All the other combinations produce other words when ONE is inserted into them i.e. bay**one**t, col**one**l, cor**one**t, h**one**sty, pi**one**er, so**one**st, swo**one**d and thr**one**s.

Verbal ability test

1   dilemma

2   banal

3   style, fashion

4   shameful, laudable

5   TACT NAIL = Atlantic

The countries are:
Portugal – gulp rota
Norway – or yawn
Bulgaria – big Laura
Argentina – regain tan

6   abeyance

slab/able, they/eyed, moan/anon, pace/cell

7   OLNEF = felon

8   erudite, ignorant

9   escalate, heighten

10   no strings attached

Numerical ability test

1   566

Multiply each number by 3 and add 2,
i.e. $188 \times 3 + 2 = 566$.

2   35 minutes i.e. 11.25

9 a.m. + $(4 \times 35 = 140)$ or 2 hours 20 minutes = 11.20.

3   Tom 60, Dick 80, Harry 100

4   9

$12 \times 8 = 96$. Similarly, $27 \times 3 = 81$ and $19 \times 4 = 76$.

5   6

6

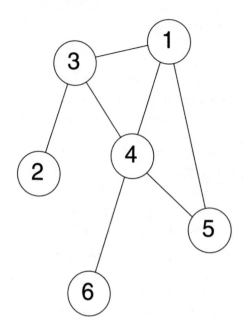

7

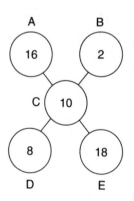

$^{A}/_{B} = D$

$A + B = E$

$E - D = C$

8   63

Explanation:

12 innings at 288 runs = 24 average
13 innings at 299 runs = 23 average (+ 11 runs)
13 innings at 351 runs = 27 average (+ 63 runs)

9   87   75   94   85   77

Explanation:

Each row is formed by adding numbers in the row above.

Column A + Column C = Column B, D + E = A, C + D = E, B + E = C, A + E = D

10   13   33

There are two alternating sequences both starting at 1. The first progresses + 3 and the second progresses + 8.

IQ test two

Spatial ability test

1

Explanation:

A is added to B to make C
C is added to D to make E
E is added to F to make G
G is added to H to make A

Similar symbols disappear.

2   B

3   2B

4   C

Explanation:

1 is added to 2 to make 3
4 is added to 5 to make 6
Similar symbols disappear.

5   G

Explanation:

A is the same as F
C is the same as D
B is the same as E

6   D

Explanation:

☐ square is completed
○ ● centre circle alternates white/black
○ right-hand circle remains
⌊ changes 90° clockwise

7   C

Explanation:

1 is added to 2 to form 3
4 is added to 5 to form 6
Similar symbols disappear.

8   B

Explanation:

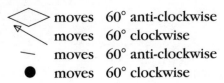

      moves   60° anti-clockwise
      moves   60° clockwise
      moves   60° anti-clockwise
      moves   60° clockwise

9   I

Explanation:

A is the same as L
B is the same as G
C is the same as J
D is the same as K
E is the same as H
F is the same as M

10   A

Explanation:

RH ● changes to ○ and moves across to left

⬭ changes to ◇

○ central circle changes colour to white

● bottom circle stays the same

❘ moves across to right and reverses

Verbal ability test

1   chamois; it is an animal, the rest are colour shades.

2   graceful, elegant

3 tin bin

4 mayonnaise

5 torpid, uplifted

6 computer literate

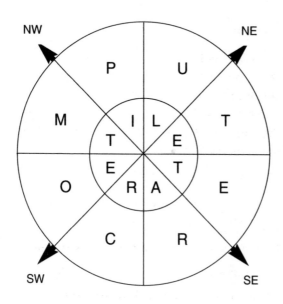

7 unmitigated, consummate

8 succinct

9 shell

10 meddle, medal

Numerical ability test

1 Infinity

2 Clarence 61
  Harold 26
  Peter 14

3 Notebook 55p
  Pencil 1p
  Book 160p
  Pen <u>80p</u>
  296p

4 XII = $_{VII}$
  XIII = $_{VIII}$

5 $8\frac{1}{4}$

  Explanation:

  $5 \times 4 = 33$ so 20 has been increased to 33.

  $\frac{33}{20} \times 5 = 8\frac{1}{4}$

6 64

7 $\left(\frac{7}{.7} \times \frac{7}{.7}\right) = 100$

8 At 1 $1\frac{1}{11}$ hrs, 2 $2\frac{2}{11}$ hrs, 3 $3\frac{3}{11}$ hrs, 4 $4\frac{4}{11}$ hrs, etc.

9 $\frac{35}{70} + \frac{148}{296} = \frac{1}{2} + \frac{1}{2} = 1$

10 $864 - 72 = 792$

Logic test

1 If they had won in 1930 I would have said, they won 6 times out of 10 times.

2

$$\frac{16}{22} \div \frac{56}{28} \div \frac{68}{17} \div \frac{26}{13} = x$$

$$\frac{16}{22} \times \frac{28}{56} \times \frac{17}{68} \times \frac{13}{26} = x$$

$$\frac{16}{22} \times \frac{1}{2} \times \frac{1}{4} \times \frac{1}{2} = x$$

$$\frac{16}{22} \times \frac{1}{16} = \frac{1}{22}$$

Explanation:

To solve problems with multiple divisions, change the division sign to a multiplication sign and reverse the numbers top on bottom, bottom on top.

3 66   66
       33
       22
        9
      $\overline{130}$ = 6 score + 10

4 7343

Explanation:

$$\text{1st digit} \begin{cases} (2) + 2^3 = & 208 \\ (3) + 3^3 = & 327 \\ (4) + 4^3 = & 464 \\ (5) + 5^3 = & 5125 \\ (6) + 6^3 = & 6216 \\ (7) + 7^3 = & 7343 \end{cases}$$

Remaining digits

5

Explanation:

2 × 6 sides
2 × 5 sided
2 × 4 sided
2 × 3 sided
2 × 2 sided (missing)
2 × 1 sided

6   3

Explanation:

18 × 9 = <u>162</u> = 2   24 × 6 = <u>144</u> = 2   30 × 2 = <u>60</u> = 3
 9 × 9 =   81   36 × 2 =   72   5 × 4 = 20

7

	ODD	EVEN	PRIME	SQUARE	CUBE
1	✓			✓	✓
2		✓	✓		
3	✓		✓		
4		✓		✓	
5	✓		✓		
6		✓			
7	✓		✓		
8		✓			✓

Only No. 6 has one tick means that the answer is 6.

8   Certainty.

9   74 kgs.

10

	S		C		H
	C	H	D		S
	S		D		
		D	S		C
C					D
		H		H	

The way forward

By now, even if you have only tackled some of the tests and puzzles in the preceding chapters, you will have given your brain a thorough work-out.

Our brain is undoubtedly our greatest asset, yet for most of us it is the part of the body that we most take for granted.

Our brain needs exercise and care in the same way as other parts of the body. We eat the right foods to keep our heart healthy, we moisturize our skin to keep it from drying out and, just as gymnasts train to improve their performance, there are exercises, or mental gymnastics, we can do to increase the performance of our brain.

Many people still have an outdated belief that there is little they can do to improve the brain they are born with and that brain cells continually degenerate with age, but, in fact, the opposite is true as cells continually develop new and stronger connections and adult brains can grow new cells, irrespective of age.

While the exercises which are contained in this book may not turn you into a genius overnight, hopefully this will be something on which you can build. If from reading this book you are convinced that it is possible to increase and maximize your brainpower, then there is a need to constantly work out your brain in order to strengthen its performance even more.

In addition to special care with nutrition and diet – the eating of a balanced diet rich in vitamins and minerals is desirable – there are several ways in which you can do this. Several of the exercises in this book are repeatable, such as thinking up different uses for everyday objects such as an elastic band or a milk bottle, and creating drawings from geometric lines. These exercises may seem trivial, but anything which puts your brain to work in a different and novel way can only be having the overall beneficial effect of activating your brain cells.

There are also other practical exercises you can carry out. Try, for example, to write out a series of instructions for performing an everyday task like boiling an egg. You might be surprised how much you need to write down to record every detail of the process. It may seem trivial, but again you are getting your mind to work in a different or novel way, in the same way that taking a different form of physical exercise stretches muscles which you did not even know existed.

In addition to the exercises suggested in Chapter 3, there are many other things you can do to improve your memory. It is essential, for example, to allow the brain to have enough sleep and rest in order for the memory to function efficiently. Also, the intake of alcohol is one of the main causes of memory loss, as alcohol interferes with short-term memory in particular, which impairs the retention of new information.

Studies have also revealed that smoking lowers the amount of oxygen reaching the brain, and this has a detrimental effect on the efficiency of memory, as well as increasing the risk of strokes and other brain-related diseases. In recent years studies among elderly smokers in Europe have revealed that they lost their ability to think, perceive and remember sooner than non-smokers, or even those who had already quit smoking.

Over the past forty years we are fortunate in that we have obtained a much greater understanding of the huge complexities of the workings of the human brain and we should be able to use this new-found knowledge considerably to our advantage. By continuously exploiting the enormous potential of our most precious asset we all have the ability to increase and maximize our brainpower, whatever our age or lifestyle. We have the ability, not just to ward off neurodegeneration, but to make more and stronger connections between our nerve cells, with the result that not only our mental but also our physical well-being will improve.

Further reading

Philip Carter and Ken Russell, *Increase Your Brainpower*, John Wiley & Sons, Chichester, 2001.

Philip Carter and Ken Russell, *IQ Testing*, John Wiley & Sons, Chichester, 2001.

Philip Carter and Ken Russell, *Psychometric Testing*, John Wiley & Sons, Chichester, 2001.

Arthur S. Reber, *The Penguin Dictionary of Psychology*, Penguin Books, Harmondsworth, 1985.

Philip Carter and Ken Russell, *Workout for a Balanced Brain*, Reader's Digest Books, London, 2001.

Peter Evans and Geoff Deehan, *The Keys to Creativity*, Grafton Books, London, 1988.

Philip Carter and Ken Russell, *More IQ Testing*, John Wiley & Sons, Chichester, 2002.

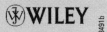